"Brian Marcel combines fascinatin
tragedies to triumphs with the key b
guided him through his successful career. Brian takes us on the
interesting journey of the barcode—one of the most revolutionary inventions of the twentieth century that is the foundation
of today's "now" economy—tracking its progress along with his
own. You don't have to be a techie to enjoy this book, just someone looking for solid strategies and useful tips to achieve your
career ambition."

—Anders Gustafsson, CEO, Zebra Technologies

"Brian Marcel has written a must-read primer for budding entrepreneurs who want to change the world, just as he has done. His
experience building a business in the barcode industry can help
readers seize opportunities and avoid pitfalls."

—Dr. Tom Hill, author of *Blessed Beyond Measure*

"In his book, *Raise the Bar, Change the Game*, Brian Marcel
reminds us how the humble barcode has changed the world and
made possible so much of the business that we now take for
granted. He has turned an everyday subject into an important
read for all budding entrepreneurs."

—Zac Goldsmith, member of Parliament
for Richmond Park and North Kingston,
London, United Kingdom

"Brian Marcel has crafted a compelling read about his successes
and failures that will resonate with all readers but especially benefit
entrepreneurs who, like him, are passionate to make their mark."

—Thomas Power, author and speaker

"Brian is well travelled in the automatic identification industry, and thus very well qualified to write this book. I encourage all who are imbued with an entrepreneurial spirit and seeking success to read *Raise the Bar, Change the Game*. This book is both *emotional* and *motivational*!"

—Richard B. Meyers, retired president,
Delta Services; chairman emeritus,
AIDC 100; and author

One of the first questions when launching anything meaningful is, "Where do I start?" If you are thinking about starting a business, this question is answered perfectly in *Raise the Bar, Change the Game*. Brian has written a brilliant primer about what it takes to start, grow, and lead a successful business that has the potential to not only change your life but to change the world.

—Jim Canfield, co-author of *CEO Tools 2.0*

RAISE THE BAR
CHANGE THE GAME

BY BRIAN MARCEL

RAISE THE BAR
CHANGE THE GAME

A SUCCESS PRIMER
FOR BUDDING ENTREPRENEURS
WHO WANT TO CHANGE THE WORLD

BY BRIAN MARCEL

Stonebrook Publishing
Saint Louis, Missouri

STONEBROOK
PUBLISHING

Edited by Nancy Erickson, The Book Professor®
TheBookProfessor.com

Library of Congress Control Number: 2018942238

Print ISBN: 978-1-7322767-2-7
eBook ISBN: 978-1-7322767-4-1
www.stonebrookpublishing.net

PRINTED IN THE UNITED STATES OF AMERICA
10 9 8 7 6 5 4 3 2 1

CONTENTS

CONTENTS

FOREWORD

Raise the Bar, Change the Game is the beautifully written autobiography of an entrepreneur. Rarely do you have a biography where personal humanity is intricately inter-woven with the business successes and failures that occur when someone takes a road never before traveled; in this case, through the newly-fallen Soviet Union. Brian Marcel and I traveled much of it in parallel, and we collaborated in Russia. Our careers had most of the same *Lessons Learned*, the summaries found at the end of each chapter that are the real value of this book.

The rapid collapse of the Soviet Union hit all of Eastern Europe like the meteor that killed the dinosaurs. Brian quotes Darwin, "It is not the strongest of the species that survives, nor the most intelligent; it is the one that is most adaptable to change." No one in Eastern Europe had a Plan B for a capitalist economy after the fall of Communism and the end of Russian domination.

Brian was tenacious. He saw that success lay in constant adaption and in coping with the old Communist mentality, while helping create a new business environment. Business became a series of transient opportunities. It was about market creation, not market fulfilment—not an easy task because business conditions were different in every city-state in Eastern Europe.

Thanks to Brian, in 1993, I was there with Sasha Maximovsky in Moscow, and trained his organization to be a Zebra Technologies reseller. As one of the first Americans in Ekaterinburg Siberia (formerly Sverdlovsk), and as Editor of ISBT128 for the International Society of Blood Transfusion, I spoke there about the new ISBT128 global barcode standard for blood at the Russian National Blood Bank meeting. I then supervised world beta-site testing there at the Sanguis Blood Bank. Together, Brian and I helped make Russia a partner in world blood banking.

This is a great book for someone who wants to be a pathfinder, a disruptor, or a change agent—not just another suit in an established firm. This book is about marketing high tech and market creation. It shares the accumulated wisdom of a true pioneer with the ease of a campfire story.

Clive P. Hohberger, PhD
Retired Vice President, Zebra Technologies Corporation
Chairman Emeritus, AIM Global

PROLOGUE

I set out to write this book about my career in the barcode industry because I'd had so many requests from fellow members of the AIDC 100 to write my memoirs. AIDC 100 is an invitation-only group of one hundred people who started the automatic identification data capture (barcode) industry and made major contributions to it over the years.

After discussions with Nancy Erickson, The Book Professor, it only took me a couple of nanoseconds to realize that the potential sales of such a book would be limited to about one hundred people—not exactly a best seller. Nancy and I chatted about how to widen the market for my book to make it a worthwhile read for young entrepreneurs who are just starting out in business. If I can, through this book, encourage them to start a business in this industry and to create exciting solutions that also change the world, I will be enormously satisfied. Great opportunities lie in new technologies that are offshoots of the barcode industry, such as the Internet of Things and blockchain technology.

I don't often think about it during my day-to-day activities, but barcodes have changed the world. In fact, the barcode is one of the most revolutionary inventions of the twentieth century. A symbol of the world's capitalism, barcode technology has changed how the world economy operates. Without barcode technology:

- Fedex couldn't guarantee overnight delivery.

- Walmart couldn't keep low prices with just-in-time logistics.

- Toyota's revolutionary Kanban manufacturing system would not exist.

Barcodes have changed the world. In fact, the barcode is one of the most revolutionary inventions of the twentieth century.

Barcodes speed up economic processes and open up new possibilities—whole new configurations that, indeed, have changed the world of business and also changed the cultural and physical landscapes we share. This simple technology has accelerated the pace of globalization, not just through the increased speed at which trade occurs, but also by enabling entire industries to take on new shapes, to inhabit new forms. The evolution of the barcode has accelerated the expansion of our global economy. From boarding passes to hospital patients, rental cars to nuclear waste, barcodes have reduced friction like few other technologies in the world's rush toward globalization.

Just about every company can benefit from a barcode solution. It enables speedy data entry without human intervention, so there are no mistakes and no paperwork. Accuracy, efficiency, and productivity improve dramatically and facilitate the introduction of best practices in a company, which goes on to change the world. I heard Sir Terry Leahy, CEO of Tesco—the third-largest retailer in the world by 1997-2011 revenues—say that without barcodes, he wouldn't have a business.

So, I can look back and say, yes, I did make a difference. I did help change the world.

I made many mistakes along the way and enjoyed some successes, too. At the end of each chapter in this book is a short paragraph about the lessons I learned at the time, some of which are discussed in more detail in the main text. My hope is that by sharing them with you, you'll be inspired to go on to greater things.

INDUSTRY BACKGROUND

If you aren't very technical, you may find the rest of this prologue rather boring, so feel free to skip it. However, it seems appropriate to explain what the barcode industry is all about and why barcodes are so important.

Our industry is called Automatic Identification and Data Capture (AIDC), although my opinion is that it should be considered part of information technology because we are the fingers of IT.

Norman Joseph Woodland is credited with the invention of the barcode as we know it. In 1948, he was approached by a graduate student at Drexel Institute of Technology in Philadelphia who had overheard the president of a local food chain, Food Fair, when he asked one of the deans to research a system that would automatically read product information during checkout. Woodland was excited and was convinced that he could develop a system to do the job. Folklore says that he went to the beach in Florida, sat in a deckchair, and fell asleep. When he woke up, his fingers traced some dots and dashes in the sand. Inspired by Morse code, he extended the dots and dashes downward, making both wide and narrow lines out of them. And so, the barcode was born.

Woodland filed for a patent that was granted in 1952, a year after he joined IBM. IBM offered to buy the patent from him but then decided it wasn't feasible to further develop it because the barcode would have to be read by something in order to process the information—and that device had not yet been invented. In 1962, Philco purchased the patent for $15,000, then sold it to RCA sometime later.

Nothing much happened until 1971, when IBM noticed a crowded exhibition booth where RCA was demonstrating a circular bulls-eye barcode—also developed by Woodland. They remembered that Woodland still worked for IBM, so they asked him to develop a standard for a uniform grocery product code for the National Association of Food Chains. Woodland then developed a stripe version of the bulls-eye, which worked far better because the printing ink didn't smudge. And so the UPC (Universal Product Code) was adopted in 1973.

NCR installed a test bed scanner at Marsh's Supermarket in Troy, Ohio, near the factory that produced the equipment. On June 26, 1974, Clyde Dawson pulled a ten-pack of Wrigley's Juicy Fruit Gum out of his basket, and handed it to Sharon Buchanan, who scanned it at 8:01 a.m. This was the first commercial use of the UPC.

———

In 1977, fewer than two hundred grocery stores scanned barcodes because 75 percent of their stock would require barcodes for the technology to be viable. A critical mass of retailers would have to install expensive scanners, and none of them wanted to move first. The big question was if the demise of the barcode, as predicted by a 1976 article in *Business Week*, would come to pass.

But analysis by stores that had installed barcode equipment showed that there were benefits other than speed of checkout. Detailed sales information that these new systems acquired allowed the stores to be more responsive to customer habits, needs, and preferences. The data showed that about five weeks after installing a scanning system, sales started to climb until they reached a 10 percent to 12 percent increase, which never dropped off.

There was also a 1 percent to 2 percent decrease in operating costs, which enabled supermarkets to lower prices, increase market share, and give shareholders a return on investment of an incredible 41.5 percent. By 1980, eight thousand stores had installed scanning equipment.

Control of the numbers encoded in the barcode was crucial to the integrity of the system. Each stock-keeping unit had to have a unique number reflecting size, color, weight, or whatever differential was appropriate. To make this happen, the United States started the UCC—or Uniform Code Council—to control the issuance of numbers. In the rest of the world, the numbering authority was the EAN (European Article Number), which was called the ANA (Article Numbering Association) in the United Kingdom. These authorities eventually morphed into GS1 in the various territories.

———

The structure of the UPC code is as follows:

- The first digit—normally a zero—indicates the product code is registered in the United States or Canada.

- Digits 2 through 6 identify the manufacturer.

- Digits 7 through 11 indicate the specific SKU (stock-keeping unit) or product code of the manufacturer.

- Digit 12, the final digit, is a check digit based on an algorithm that ensures there's been no transposition of numbers.

- Outside the United States, it is called EAN 13 because there is a thirteenth number to accommodate the global country codes.

The thick and thin lines—and the spaces between them—represent ones and zeros in the binary system. They're read by a red laser scanner that *reflects* light from the spaces and *absorbs* light from the bars. Thus, the beam times how long it "sees" light or dark and translates that information into a character. The bars must be printed in black, blue, green, or brown, and the spaces in white, red, yellow, or orange to create sufficient contrast for the laser to differentiate the bars.

UPC and EAN are called *one-dimensional symbologies.* There are many other symbologies, such as Code 39, which is alpha numeric rather than numeric; EAN 128, which encodes alpha-numeric upper and lower case; and ASCII codes, used in the supply chain for pallets. There are also two-dimensional barcodes that are printed in squares that can encode up to one thousand bytes of data, such as signatures, photos, and fingerprints. They're used on ID cards and driver's licenses.

Another favorite symbology is the QR code—or quick response code—invented in 1994 for the Japanese automobile industry to track vehicles in manufacturing. The QR code has wider popularity now because it contains a large amount of data and can be blown up into a huge symbol that can be scanned by a smartphone camera. There are so many symbologies in use now that it's best to look up any others that might be of interest.

———

In Eastern Europe, which is where we are a market leader, it wasn't wise to focus on one particular vertical market because this was an emerging market. Our solutions assist these industries:

- Retail

- Manufacturing

- Transportation and logistics

- Warehouse management and distribution

- Government

- Health care

- Hospitality

Our main applications are:

Inventory Management: These solutions are implemented across industries and use barcodes to keep very accurate stock records that ensure customers will have the item they want, when they want it. Retailers reduce the lines at the checkout by scanning the barcode, which not only looks up the product description and the price in the database, but also removes that item from the stock file, triggering a stock-replenishment order.

Supply Chain: These solutions benefit from barcodes on containers placed on pallets, where cases of product are scanned and tracked as they pass through checkpoints and hubs of carriers. With the advent of the Internet of Things and RFID (radio-frequency identification) sensors, it's now possible to track the temperature changes to a shipment, as well as if and where it was dropped and damaged.

Warehouse Management: These solutions include all warehouse operations, from goods received to shipping and stocktaking. Sometimes the customer wants real-time data; for example, if the goods received are immediately needed on the shop floor, they can be sent directly there, rather than being moved into stock. This feature saves our customers two or three days of potential delays.

Field Service Management: With these applications, engineers receive their daily tasks on hand-held terminals that guide them to the location where something needs repair. They can look up the repair history online and download plans to make the repair.

Asset Management: These solutions track assets like furniture, files, or whatever asset needs to be tracked. The information indicates the item's value and history, forming an audit trail.

Retail: These solutions track the movement of goods into a super-market, price verification, inventory management, and checkout on a smartphone.

Manufacturing: These solutions allow the business to track items during manufacture, to assemble parts, and to manage tasks throughout the factory.

Government: Such solutions track postal workers on their routes, issue passenger tickets on the railways, track and schedule main-tenance of heavy machinery, and issue voter and ID cards.

Health Care: These solutions track blood from donor to patient to make sure patients get the right blood and drugs at the proper time. They also identify patients as they travel around the hospi-tal, maintain electronic patient records, and track X-rays.

Hospitality: These solutions allow mobile check-in to hotels and airlines, and manage delegates at conferences and exhibitions.

———

RFID tags were once hyped to replace barcodes because they don't require line-of-sight to be read. However, they are quite expensive compared to a barcode, which is more or less cost-free. RFID tags are silicon chips that have a copper aerial attached. The most common applications are:

- Animal tracking

- Collecting motorway tolls

- Tracking expensive item-level inventory such as suits, to make sure trouser and jacket sizes match and are always available

- Materials management

- Access control

- Tracking books in library systems

- Laundry management

- Real-time location and yard management

- Internet of Things: sensors on consumer goods, machines, and pretty much everything are connected to the Internet and send data 24/7 to the cloud, which is analyzed so quick business decisions can be made.

———

This brief overview of the industry should shed some light on how these applications have changed the world thus far and will continue to do so. What started with barcodes has morphed into complex technological solutions that are revolutionizing all aspects of life and commerce. It's an ever-expanding industry that invites creativity and innovation and promises a bright and lucrative future for those who dare to enter.

My hope is that you will be inspired to create your own solutions so you, too, can change the world. I believe the best is yet to come!

1 THE START BEFORE THE START

always wanted to start my own company, but I had no idea what that company might be. In fact, at eighteen years old, I had no special interests, although I did have A-level qualifications in French, German, and Italian. So, I took a vocational guidance course, which consisted of multiple-choice questions that were analyzed by a computer. As it turned out, my aptitudes were maths, sales, business activities, and accounts. Other interests included administration and any occupation dependent upon persuasion, such as sales or politics. I also scored above average in writing. The course included an interview with a consultant, who highlighted my most likely path to greatness. He told me to steer away from farming and suggested I might enjoy law or possibly management.

Although the results weren't really decisive as far as my direction was concerned, they gave me self-confidence. They showed me how I could pursue the best likely outcomes and unveiled my potential talent, which had, up to that point, remained hidden. A good friend of mine had also taken the course, and the consultant recommended that he go into the film industry. He got a job with Walt Disney and thrived, which confirmed the credibility of the tests.

In the meantime, my parents sent me off to Paris to work for a friend in the soundproofing business as an apprentice. I could hardly call it work. I spent ten hours a day making tea and photocopies, so I didn't learn much in terms of business. I did, however, hone my French language skills—in which I am still fluent—and I studied marketing at the Sorbonne for three weeks, which was quite productive.

And I had a ball in Paris! I was dating an American girl, and one day she suggested something that only the young would ever consider.

"Let's go to Place Pigalle tonight and dress Brian as a prostitute," Bridget said to our group of friends. "He would look great in my dress, and we could have fun making him up!'

"You can't be serious!" I said. "A prostitute has to wear stiletto heels, and there's no way I'll do that. I would feel like an absolute idiot."

"Come on. Please?" her friend Jane said. "It will be such fun!"

So, I capitulated. They made me up with garish makeup, and I wore Bridget's provocative clothes, lips daubed with thick red lipstick, and feet clad in her high heels.

Off we drove to Place Pigalle, the center of nightlife in Paris—and where most "ladies of the night" hung out.

They dropped me off opposite a shady doorway outside a small block of apartments that could well belong to one of those ladies. I stumbled out of the car and tottered over to the doorway, making a dive for the wall to stop myself from falling over. My friends drove away, convulsing in hysterics, and took up a vantage point on the opposite side of the street. I stood in the doorway, adopted what I hoped was a suggestive pose, and waited to see what happened.

Nothing happened for half an hour until a large man with a moustache and beret sidled up to me and asked in French:

"Combien la nuit, chérie?" *What do you charge for the night?*

What on earth was I to do? I was cornered; so, being a quick thinker, I said to him:

"Chéri, let me go and ask my boss how much to charge you—maybe get a special rate for you, hein? Go to the end of the street, and I will have an answer for you when you get back."

To my huge relief, he bought this and turned away and started walking.

The moment he got some distance away, I made a fast exit and disappeared around the corner, where my friends picked me up. I escaped!

———

When I returned to London from Paris, my mother decided that my career would be in her father's brokerage firm. Another partner's son had already joined the firm, and she worried that he might inherit it rather than me. They took me on, and I learned the business—or at least I tried.

SETBACKS

One day four years later, the senior partner called me into his office and said, "Brian you've been here four years. It's quite clear that you don't always manage to get the best deals on the floor, as you lack the ability to build relationships in the market. It might be best if you found another career path because you don't seem very suited to this one! Your grandfather is sad that the stock market doesn't seem to be the right fit for you."

In other words, I got fired—from my own grandfather's business! Mother was not pleased, and I was so ashamed.

So, what was next for the intrepid entrepreneur? I thought I might try my hand at commerce, since institutions hadn't seemed to work out. After all, the vocational guidance course had recommended that I work for a large commercial firm.

My father ran an haute couture dress business in a shop in

Knightsbridge, the fashionable part of London, but his business didn't interest me. However, he had many business connections and arranged an interview with the overseas director at Wiggins Teape, one of the more famous paper manufacturers. They employed 22,000 people across forty-two countries, and they agreed to take me on for a two-year training program with the intent that I would be posted to one of their locations overseas. Would it be a plum spot like Australia, or would it be a dump like Lagos? I was fortunate; I was assigned to South Africa, where the company was called Alex Pirie & Sons. I made my way there in 1970, on a British Airways DC 10 at the tender age of twenty-four.

I couldn't help but make fabulous friends and live the life of Riley. I had servants, a swimming pool, and plenty of golf. And I had a great time at work. My first job was as a tea boy—definitely the bottom rung of the ladder—which I'm happy to say didn't last too long. Soon, I became a salesman and covered the whole of South Africa, a vast country. I drove tens of thousands of kilometers in various Ford Cortinas over the years, selling high-quality papers.

We made a paper called Readaspeed that had a very smooth surface coating and could pass through the IBM 1275, a high-speed sorting machine. It read printed numbers on utility bills with a cathode ray tube similar to the tube in a TV. As a result of this exposure, I became very interested in computers and friendly with the buyer at IBM, who bought tons of the paper.

We soon added carbonless copying paper to our portfolio of products, which eliminated the need for messy carbon paper. I successfully targeted continuous business forms manufacturers which, up until that point, had to put reels of carbon paper between the forms they printed that fed through the high-speed computer printers of that time.

As a successful salesman, they next sent me to our label printing division in Cape Town, where I met my gorgeous soon-to-be-wife, Liz Bruce-Brown from Durban. This is where we printed the wine of origin seal, a statutory label that authenticated wine. This necessitated multiple visits to all the wine estates to discuss their statutory needs, and I thought I had the best job in the world!

After a year or so, I went back to Johannesburg to be marketing manager for the fine papers division; we sold high-quality printing and writing papers like Conqueror, the best-known brand. It was at one of my promotional events that I got fired for a second time.

It happened at the annual advertising awards competition, which Alex Pirie & Sons had entered to promote one of their brands of fine papers. Our entry included a rather glamorous young lady—a colleague from our Cape Town office. I hired a local composer to write some music and got a dance professional to teach her a routine. My idea was for her to appear on stage wrapped in the promoted paper from head to toe, wearing nothing underneath. When she finished the dance routine, she let some of the paper slip, exposing strategic parts of her anatomy.

You can imagine what happened in a theater full of male advertising executives! We won first prize.

And I got fired.

My boss, the marketing director, called me in the next morning. I thought he was going to congratulate me.

"Brian," he said, "I know you won last night, but it was in very bad taste. Alex Pirie cannot be associated with nudity on stage and such a tasteless piece of work. I think it appropriate for you to move on. Maybe it's time for you to return to England and pursue a career there."

This was a huge shock to me. I had expected a heap of praise, not the firing squad.

FINDING MY WAY

It was time to return to England. I applied for two jobs, one at an insurance company in London and the other at Spicer Cowan, a paper merchant owned by Reed International that was even bigger than Wiggins Teape. Both companies offered me the same salary, and I had to decide which one to take. Spicer Cowan won out because of my skills and experience in paper.

After a few months, I was asked to join a small division called *national accounts,* which was run by one of the directors. It was really just a fancy name for a small department that had only one product—printing paper from a small Portuguese mill. There were only three of us in the department, and we were tasked to sell tons of this stuff to national accounts.

It didn't take long before I got bored being a one-product pony, so I asked my boss if he would mind if I looked around for something else to sell. He agreed.

> **It didn't take long before I got bored being a one-product pony, so I asked my boss if he would mind if I looked around for something else to sell.**

I wanted to visit the commercial departments of the various foreign embassies to identify countries that had paper mills that weren't yet represented in the UK. After visiting seven such embassies with no luck, I got fed up. When the German consul gave me the same sad story—that they had no unrepresented German paper mills—I answered.

"OK," I said, "I understand that there are no German paper mills without UK representation. Is there anything *else* you have on your books that you don't know what to do with?"

"Yes," he said after a moment's hesitation. The consul went to a large drawer in the corner of the room and started rummaging through some papers. After a minute or two, he turned around and brandished a green-and-white brochure.

"This has been on my desk for a year. It's from a company in Augsburg called Datronic, and I can't find anyone who's interested in it. What do you think?"

I looked at it and saw some barcodes highlighted within the text. It seemed this company manufactured pieces of film on which they plotted a barcode, which printers used for printing onto retail products. They called them Film Masters.

I later learned that the barcode had to be plotted onto the film with .005 mm accuracy to allow for any ink spread when the label was printed—which could interfere with the label's scanability at the checkout. This required special equipment.

My interest was aroused. I connected a few dots: computers, paper, printing, barcodes—the connection was obvious.

"Yes," I said, "I am very interested. Thank you very much."

I left the embassy with the brochure and felt like I'd found something new we could sell. It made sense to promote these Film Masters to our current customers that already printed retail product labels. I hoped my boss would see the same potential.

He did, indeed, buy into my vision and gave me full permission to pursue the opportunity. I phoned Datronic that same day—there was no email back then—and said we would like to represent their company in the UK. They flew over the following week, and we were accepted as their UK agent. The next month they trained me for three days in Augsburg, Germany.

At that time, there were only five companies in the business, which meant we could make a big splash. Our price was the same as the competition's, and because each product and product variable—as well as the boxes for multiple quantities of product—needed a unique barcode number, it was very profitable.

I captured 14 percent of the market share in year one through grit and hard work. I went to supermarkets and scoured the shelves to find products that didn't have barcodes. Then I contacted those manufacturers to offer our services. Slowly but surely, I built a base of business.

I captured 14 percent of the market share in year one through grit and hard work.

It was 1979, only four years after the first store in the UK, Fine Fare in Spalding, had adopted scanning technology. They had determined that to make scanning economical, at least 80 percent of all products should have barcodes. The market was huge.

LESSONS LEARNED:

- If you get fired, it's not the end of the world. Just pick yourself up after a bit of self-analysis and move on. I believe that everything that happens is meant to be and is for the best—and how right I've been! If I hadn't been fired from my grandfather's firm, I wouldn't have gone to South Africa and met my wife, Liz. If I hadn't been fired from Alex Pirie and returned to England, I wouldn't have gone into the barcoding industry.

- It's never too late. At this point, I was already thirty-five years old, and I had yet to discover what sort of company I wanted to start. I always knew I wanted to start my own company but never knew what I wanted to do. So, I kept following the opportunities until they led me to something that appealed to me.

- You must recognize opportunity when it presents itself. Don't make excuses and say that the timing is wrong or that you don't have the money. Opportunities in life are few and far between, and you must grab each one as it comes. You won't get another chance.

QUESTIONS FOR YOU:

- Think of something dramatic that happened in your work life that knocked you back. How did you react? Did it shake your self-confidence for a short time? How did you pick yourself up? What did you learn from your mistakes? Can you think of anything positive that came from it?

- Do you want to start your own company? Do you know what business you want to be in? What are you very passionate about?

- Think of an opportunity that you missed. Why didn't you seize it? Do you have any regrets? What could you have done differently?

2 BEGIN WITH A PLAN

So, you're desperate to be your own boss, but how do you make that transition from employee to self-employed? You want to make a difference in the world, but how and where do you start? If all the original ideas have been taken, how do you disrupt existing markets?

Why not borrow someone else's idea and do what they do—but better? This leaves the playing field wide open and allows you to stretch your mind and imagination.

Start by taking a blank sheet of paper and writing down the things that you're passionate about. You'll have a better chance of being successful if you're passionate about the subject because there will be many ups and downs and hard knocks that you'll have to deal with over the years. Without passion and a strong belief in what you do, it's easy to give up when the going gets tough.

At some point, you'll probably present your idea to a friend, family member, or colleague who will pour cold water on it and say that it won't work or that it's been done before. These people give off negative vibes. They're naysayers who've never built a successful company. Do NOT listen to them! Take to heart the immortal words of Sir Richard Branson: "Screw it; let's do it!"

Belief in yourself and confidence are crucial. Ninety-five percent of people lack self-confidence, which means that only 5 percent have it. Self-confidence allows you to see the big picture and will motivate you to see things through and ignore the naysayers. You need a positive attitude.

> **Belief in yourself and confidence are crucial. Self-confidence allows you to see the big picture and will motivate you to see things through and ignore the naysayers.**

Do not, however, confuse self-confidence with arrogance. Being arrogant is not a good characteristic.

I'm sure you've heard of the Law of Attraction, which states that if you put out positive vibes, the universe will respond and send back positive things and people. The opposite is also true: negativity begets negativity, so beware!

BRAINSTORM

Once you know what you're passionate about, write down a BHAG—a big hairy audacious goal. This is a dream that describes what your business will look like in five years, ten years, and twenty years down the line. Use a blank sheet of paper to allow your mind to wander. You can achieve anything, so dream and dream big.

Sit down by yourself or with your team to do some Blue Ocean Strategy thinking using colored Post-it notes. Write down seven things you are passionate about, and put the notes in a row across the top of a piece of flip-chart paper. Next, create new notes for the businesses you could start from these seven things. Create columns by placing the business notes underneath the passion it belongs to. You can use this methodology to brainstorm anything.

This is different from Red Ocean Strategy—which your competitors do—where they choose between a low-cost or high-value model and come up with products/services to satisfy a niche market. Your strategy will help you choose a low-cost *and* a high-value model and exploit commonalities between customers and noncustomers.

Next, figure out if you're going to disrupt somebody's market. Draw a strategy canvas (see illustration on the next page) that includes factors in their value chain. Plot them on a graph to indicate whether they merit high or low value to the model. When you decide which factors to eliminate and reduce and which to raise and create, you'll have a new and disruptive business model.

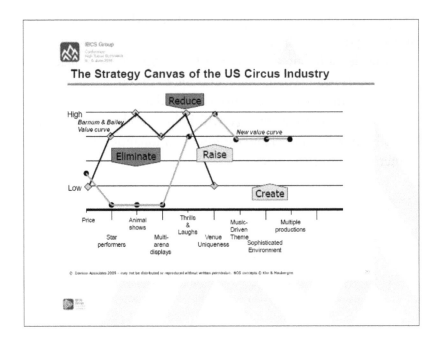

As Stephen Covey says in his book *The Seven Habits of Highly Effective People*, "begin with the end in mind." Imagine what your business will look like in the future, work backward from your BHAG to today, and you'll see how you need to start and grow.

MAKE A PLAN

Next, you need a plan, but not a fifty-page business plan—unless you need to pitch to outside investors who may not understand your business. This is just for you, and you can probably get it on one sheet of paper.

I was first introduced to this idea by author Kraig Kramers. His original book, *CEO Tools*, has been updated and revised as *CEO Tools 2.0* by Jim Canfield and Kraig Kramers. Here's an example of a blank 1-Page Business Plan:

Your Company Name
Business Plan Name

1-Page Business Plan

Vision. *Describe the business you will build (in a few well-constructed sentences).*

Mission Statement. *Describe the purpose, focusing on benefits for the customer.*

Competitive Advantage: *Use numbers that can be authenticated*

Objectives. *First, sales; second, profitability; no more than 6-8 "SMART" objectives: specific, measurable, action-oriented, include results, time-delimited.*
-
-
-
-
-

Strategies. *Statements that set direction, philosophy, values, and methodology for building the business and managing the enterprise. Use 4-6 core strategies common to the industry.*
-
-
-
-

Plans. *Business-building or infrastructure-building action steps necessary to implement the overall plan. Include completion date.*

"What about getting outside investors?" you might say. Apart from family and friends or the need to buy expensive equipment or samples, forget about the money. If you don't have it, there are multiple and sometimes audacious ways to get it.

Wait: Do I hear you thinking, *I can't do it without money!*

Actually, you can. Do what you have to do, in order to get the start-up capital you need. Ask friends and family for a loan, ask the bank for a small loan or line of credit, use your credit card, mortgage your home. Ask your suppliers for credit, and make sure your debtors/customers pay you up front or at least before you have to pay your suppliers/creditors. Get your cash *in* before it has to go *out* and keep as much of it as possible. You'll learn that cash is king and is the most important measurement in business. You can make a one million dollar profit, but with no cash—perhaps because customers are not paying you or you have overextended yourself—you'll go bust! Measure your cash position at least once per month, or even once per day if appropriate.

Your plan should start with a vision statement. What is your vision for the company? Next write a purpose statement: What is the purpose of your company? Try these little benchmark tests every time you make a decision:

1. Does it pass the So-What test? When you think of an idea, ask yourself, "So what?" In other words, does it change the world, achieve a goal, etc. If you have a positive answer, then the idea is validated. If not, then forget it.

2. Does it pass the WIIFM test—What's In It For Me?—from the customer's standpoint?

3. If it fails either of these tests, then take a different path.

Next write down your competitive advantage. Why should anyone want to buy from you?

The next sections are the goals, strategies, and actions for the first year, which you can modify as the year progresses. Start with five goals, then five strategies to achieve those goals. Write down the actions needed to carry out the strategies. Remember to write down the *name* of the person who's accountable to get it done with the due date.

Every goal and strategy must be SMART, in other words Specific, Measurable, Achievable, Realistic, Time-based. Thus, a goal that says you'll be the biggest company in the world is not SMART in both senses of the word. Instead, say you want to achieve sales of one million dollars by the end of this fiscal year.

> *Every goal and strategy must be SMART, in other words Specific, Measurable, Achievable, Realistic, Time-based.*

At the end of my first year of selling Film Masters, I got bored again, so I asked Datronic, the German company we represented, if they would support me if I went out on my own. Unfortunately, they would not agree. But as luck would have it, an American pioneer in the Film Master imaging field called Photographic Sciences asked me to set up their company in the UK, and I agreed.

We had a pretty good setup. Mary, my second employee, worked from home. She took the orders by phone and placed them with a competitor, Numeric Arts, which made the Film Masters for us. Our customers insisted on next-day delivery, so I employed a friend who lived near Numeric Arts to go there every afternoon and collect the orders, address and pack the Film Masters into jiffy bags, and then post them. Our overhead was minimal, and it was very profitable.

One day a rich investment banker named Jack Hickman—Black Jack, as he was nicknamed—invested his money in Photographic Sciences. He wanted to become their chairman; he had delusions of grandeur. He promoted me to managing director and opened a posh office in Hill Street, Mayfair—a very fancy part of London. Hickman called this his international headquarters from where he would take over the world.

Our first meeting felt like something out of the movies. We met at the Ritz Hotel in Mayfair for lunch. I walked into the dining room and wondered who on earth this man was who was flashing his money around at the Ritz. He got up to greet me. He was a stocky man, a bit shorter than I was, and he wore an immaculate morning suit, complete with white shirt and grey tie. What was most striking was his hair—jet black and slicked back with hair cream. He looked like a smooth investment banker, which is exactly what he was.

"Brian," he said, "we are very pleased with what you do for us, and I want you to take over the UK company. You'll be our managing director and will move into a new HQ in Hill Street, Mayfair. After lunch, we'll go see the office and discuss a plan."

Lunch was very pleasant. Hickman talked about himself most of the time, which suited me because I was still in a state of shock at his appearance, which was a bit overwhelming.

The office was in a beautiful building that looked like a house. My office had double wooden doors, which led to an enormous space with a huge desk and some comfortable armchairs. Behind the desk, glass doors opened onto a beautiful garden with a terrace that must have been at least seventy feet long, which in Mayfair was huge and unusual. In fact, this office was over-the-top in the same vein as Hickman, but not in keeping with the size of the company, which was only four people.

On his visits to London, he spent several days at a time at the Ritz Hotel and travelled around in a chauffeur-driven Mercedes. Not a problem for me, of course, as I was more than happy to travel in style and eat at the Ritz from time to time.

One day, Hickman suggested that we make appointments with some of my connections in Europe that had similar businesses. We travelled around and explored opportunities to build a network of companies with ours at the epicenter. Hickman's message was very visionary. He wanted to bundle all the elements of barcoding—Film Masters, label printers, scanners, hand-held terminals, and software—into one solution that we would market to large international companies like Exxon and Wal-Mart.

I didn't understand this total solution concept at all, and neither did any of the people we pitched to, so the whole thing fell flat. It's too bad that Hickman was ahead of his time because this is exactly what we've done since the 1990s.

Hickman also wanted to buy a barcode labeling company called Harland Data Systems in Beverley in the north of England—a good four-hour drive from London. I was supposed to keep an eye on it for him and represent our interests. (Managing the company was unnecessary because they already had a very good managing director.) Hickman often flew over from New York, and we drove up there together for board meetings.

After eight months or so, Harland started to have problems meeting their targets. Panic. Now Hickman flew over more often. We'd drive up to Harland's offices together, have a meeting, and drive back the same night. Then Hickman would fly back to the States the next day, only to return a couple of days later. This cycle was repeated again and again. And I was exhausted!

In the end, Harland went bust, which caused big financial problems for Photographic Sciences in the States. It put them into Chapter 11 bankruptcy, which protected them from their creditors while they restructured.

As a result, Photographic Sciences closed its UK office, and I was no longer needed. They allowed me to take the customer base I'd built up and the company car, a nice BMW 535. That was the end of Photographic Sciences UK but the beginning of my company, Bar Code Systems! In November 1982, I started Bar Code Systems (BCS) at age thirty-seven. And I never looked back.

In November 1982, I started Bar Code Systems (BCS) at age thirty-seven. And I never looked back.

Hickman was, indeed, a visionary, and he was inspirational in many ways. He was a larger-than-life character, but there was also a seamy side to him, as I later learned. Apparently, there were irregularities in his investment banking business, and he got thrown in jail and committed suicide at a young age.

LESSONS LEARNED:

So far, every significant move in my life was *reactive* rather than *proactive*. But I succeeded because I learned to grab every opportunity, which is what you need to do, too.

- Being reactive can work, but it's much better to be proactive.

- Don't listen to naysayers. Press ahead with your dreams and say, "Screw it; let's do it!"

- Begin with the end in mind.

- Have a one-page business plan that includes:
  - Vision Statement
  - Purpose Statement
  - So-What Test
  - WIIFM Test
  - Competitive advantage
  - Five SMART Goals (Specific, Measurable, Achievable, Realistic, Time-based)
  - BHAG (Big Hairy Audacious Goal)
  - Five Strategies
  - Actions with timeline and person accountable to carry out these strategies to achieve the goals.

- Be positive. Don't surround yourself with negative people.

QUESTIONS:

- Do you consider yourself to be proactive or reactive? Which do you prefer? Should you change?

- Did you ever have a good idea but was told it wouldn't work? How many times? By whom? How did it make you feel? Can you revisit that idea now and execute it?

- Can you think of someone in your life whose glass is always half empty rather than half full? What effect do they have on you? Can you get that person out of your life or at least sideline them? How would things change if you did?

3 *HIRE THE BEST PEOPLE*

One of the most important things you can do for your business is to hire the best people you can find. From the very beginning, you must overcome the temptation to put up with mediocre people because you'll need to rely on a whole team to grow your business.

A pattern develops when you hire mediocre staff. They pass through three phases during their first six to twelve months:

> **One of the most important things you can do for your business is to hire the best people you can find.**

1. Faith: When you first hire them, you have faith that they will perform.

2. Hope: They haven't performed yet, but you still hope they will.

3. Charity: If they still underperform, you don't want to pay them, so it just becomes a gift to charity!

Make sure you're never in that situation. You must hire people who will perform to the standard of excellence that you demand!

HOW TO FIND GOOD PEOPLE

How do you find these people? The obvious route is a recruitment agency, but their commission is typically 20 percent of the new hire's annual salary. You can advertise online through sites like ZipRecruiter or monster.com or through social media such as LinkedIn. But all of these methods require you to consider unknown applicants; if, however, you know the person—or know of them—the risk is much lower.

Your first stop should be the competition. Maybe you've run across one of their salespeople who always beats you to an order. Hire him or her!

Exhibitions are another fertile ground. Watch people at their booths to see how they behave and interact with visitors. Pretend to be a prospect and test them yourself. If it's the wrong time for you to hire anyone, put the individual's card in your file and pull it out when you're ready to add someone new.

You can also use a headhunter to search for a profile that meets your specifications. They may not have such a person on their books, but they'll call companies that may have someone similar and try to persuade them to leave. Knowing this, our receptionist had strict instructions not to speak with anyone who she suspected was calling to entice our staff away!

THE INTERVIEW PROCESS

Interviewing potential employees requires a special skill set. Some interviewers make up their minds in the first thirty seconds, one way or another. They call it "gut feeling." Most of the time it will be the wrong decision. Make a rule for yourself: no matter what your gut tells you, you'll give the person at least thirty minutes before you make a judgment. A wet-fish hand-shake does tend to put me off because the interviewee will never be assertive, which is an important characteristic expected from an employee. Nonetheless, I still give the person thirty minutes of my time.

Toyota holds five days of interviews with candidates and makes them travel to different factories. If you don't have the time for that, you can find out a great deal about someone in ninety minutes.

It's important to ask open-ended questions, questions that can't be answered "yes" or "no." Keep in mind the specific behaviors you are looking for. Be sure that at least one-third of your questions pertain to the qualifications for the job, one-third are about their track record, and the final and most important third probe how the person will fit in with the company. You set the values and direction for the company and should expect the behaviors of everyone on the team to align with your culture, values, and company goals.

You set the values and direction for the company and should expect the behaviors of everyone on the team to align with your culture, values, and company goals.

In the interview, ask candidates what three things they are most proud of in their business or personal life. Ask about their three biggest business successes and what they would do again if they had the chance. Ask a few open-ended questions to explore whether they have the behaviors you want such as:

- If you couldn't be a salesman, what would you be?

- Everyone has strengths and weaknesses. When we are open and admit our weakness that allows us to grow and is a sign of strength. So, what's the one critical area that has caused you some problems that you'd like to change?

- Have you ever been motivated—even consumed—by a task or a job? Tell me about it.

- Values and character are developed early in youth, sometimes as a result of an important family situation—even a crisis. What are some of your important values and how were they formed?

- Microsoft has a great interview question: Why is a manhole cover round? It's a problem-solving question used to test how a person approaches a problem with more than one possible answer. It tests their logic and common sense. There are several answers, and you can accept any that make sense. (*See more interview questions in appendix B.*)

If you like the person, have others on the team interview them. You may also want one of their future colleagues to meet with them.

Next, invite the candidate to dinner to see how they behave after a few drinks. Ask, "If you ordered a steak and it came well-cooked when you wanted it rare, what would you do about it?" If they say they'd attract the waitress, berate her, and tell her to take it back, they'd be out!

When your business is a bit larger, you can afford to hire people you don't need right away. In his fantastic book *Good to Great*, author Jim Collins says to imagine that you are the driver of a bus, which is a metaphor for your company. Make sure the bus is going in the right direction and then put the people on the bus. It doesn't matter what seat they take. Just get them on the bus and worry about where they should sit later.

———

I started Bar Code Systems (BCS) in 1982. BCS had just two employees, me and my late wife, Liz. I relied on Liz to challenge my decisions, which opened my mind up to alternatives. She was compassionate in situations regarding the staff, and most of the time she was right. We had a great mutual trust and, for the most part, I allowed her to persuade me to do things her way. We built up the company together, and I was lucky to have her because an entrepreneur's life is a lonely one. You need someone to bounce ideas off and get feedback in a frank way. Liz was free from hidden agendas, so I trusted her.

We worked initially from our flat in Barnes, London, above a Kentucky Fried Chicken franchise, but after a year or so we decided to move to a house in East Sheen. At the time, nobody'd ever heard of East Sheen because it was on the "wrong side" of the River Thames. Our first employee was our office manager, Christine. In 1986, we hired our first salesperson.

One morning at 9:00 a.m. sharp, the front doorbell rang, and I went downstairs to answer it.

When I opened the door, my mouth nearly fell open. There stood a gorgeous young girl with shortish blonde hair and emerald green eyes. She stood about five feet five inches tall and was quite tanned. She wore a red blouse and dark skirt.

"Good morning," she said. "Are you Brian? I'm Judith Green, and I've come for an interview for the sales job."

I was surprised by her Midlands accent, which was quite broad but not unattractive. In fact, the whole package was quite attractive! Her handshake was firm, and I ushered her in. I wondered what on earth Liz would say when she saw her.

"Sit down and I'll get you a coffee. Let me introduce you to my wife, Liz."

Liz showed no emotion at all, and it wasn't till a few years later that she confessed that she had been very jealous and wary of Judith. I won't deny that Judith and I developed a bond, but not in a sexual way. We both respected the boundaries.

We interviewed Judith and she met all our requirements, so we hired her and started her training. This was her first job out of school, so she came cheap, but she picked things up very fast. It was a good hire.

Judith accompanied me on customer visits but couldn't understand why we crammed so much into each day. We saw five customers each day. Our pattern was to arrive for the first appointment at 9:00 a.m. when the customer started work. Our next appointment was at 10:30, then another at 12:00 p.m. In the afternoon, we started at 2:00 p.m. and had our last appointment at 4:00 p.m.

Because we covered the whole of the UK, on some days we had to leave home at 6:00 a.m. to get to the first customer by 9:00 a.m., and we might not be back home before 9:00 p.m. This required a detailed travel plan. There were no satellite navigation systems in those days, but Judith took to it like a duck to water. In the first year, she sold £250,000, she sold £450,000 the second year, and we reached our first £1 million in 1988, just five years after we started up.

One evening while I was still at the office, Judith phoned me, in tears.

"I was at the hospital, and they found a lump in my breast the size of a golf ball," she sobbed.

"Where are you now?" I whispered, in total shock.

"At Bruno's Cafe on High Street."

"I'll be right there."

I dropped everything and dashed over. She sat at a table, her huge green eyes awash with tears. She looked so young and frail. I couldn't help myself, and I sat down and wept with her. We held hands as she explained how she had found the lump and went to get a checkup.

How could this happen to one so young? It was so unfair. Twelve months later, at age thirty-two, she passed away. I visited her bedside many times and, at her request, was with her in her last moments. We held hands while she breathed her last.

What a brilliant salesperson she was, and we'd had such a great connection. Her husband, however, wouldn't talk to me after the funeral. He blamed me for putting so much stress on her that she got breast cancer. That was OK; he felt he needed to take his loss out on me. We both hurt badly.

Who knows if he may have been right? Later, Liz also got breast cancer and died, as did my wonderful assistant, Valda, after working with me for more than a decade. Was I cursed? Were *they* cursed because they worked for me?

Our staff performed very well, and they enjoyed our culture, which allowed them to make mistakes without fear of punishment. If you have a fear-of-failing culture, your people will be afraid to experiment. Innovation will never happen, and you'll end up being a copy of the competition.

> **If you have a fear-of-failing culture, your people will be afraid to experiment. Innovation will never happen, and you'll end up being a copy of the competition.**

LESSONS LEARNED:

- Hone your interview skills. Don't make a gut decision in the first thirty seconds, even if the candidate has a characteristic you don't like.

- Ask open-ended questions to bring out the behaviors you want to see. Then you'll be able to predict whether they have the right chemistry to fit in with the team.

- If you can afford it, get the right person on the bus even if you don't have the right seat for them yet.

- Keep track of the good people you meet. Even the waitress who serves you in a restaurant may have the qualities you want.

- Keep in mind that past performance predicts future performance.

- Lead a culture of innovation and excellence, and you will attract top candidates to your company.

Earlier, I suggested that stealing an employee from a competitor was a good start for recruiting, and it often is, but you must be careful. If they're in sales, they won't always bring their customers with them. Even though the customer purchased from *them*, they also bought from their *company*, and that may be where their loyalties lie.

QUESTIONS FOR YOU:

- Remember some of the interviews you've conducted. Try to pick out what was good and what was bad about them, so you can learn from it.

- How would you rate your interview skills?

- Have you ever made snap judgments in an interview? Did any of those first impressions turn out to be wrong?

- How many people have you hired that you regret hiring? Are any of your employees currently in "charity" mode?

4 FOCUS ON PROFITS

The Film Master business was, in many ways, a cash cow. There were only about six serious players in the UK and plenty of business to go around. I could buy the Film Masters for about £5 and sold them for £15. This worked out well for a few years.

We started BCS in our flat, but after a couple of years, we moved into a house on top of which I built a loft conversion, which became my office. That lasted only a couple of years until we moved to our first office in Nikon House, Ham in Richmond-upon-Thames. I rented half the ground floor from Nikon, which owned the rest of the building. It was very new and posh, so we were very proud to have expanded to our first "grown-up" office.

CHANGE THE GAME

Our market share was quite good by this time—around 1985—and I was looking for ways to increase profits. I'd been purchasing the Film Masters from a third party because there were only three manufacturers in the world that produced what was called a Film Master Generator. These generators were specialized plotting machines that were calibrated to a high level and designed to make Film Masters to meet the requirements of an entire country. The Codemaster was the best and was made in the States, but there was one already installed at Kings Town Photocodes in Beverley. Symbol Technologies also made a machine in the States, which Numeric Arts bought; and Axicon, an English company, made a machine called a Microplotter. No manufacturer would sell their machine to more than one company per country, so I couldn't buy an actual machine. I would have to buy the Film Masters from one of these competitors at a higher price than if I owned a machine. I chose to work with Numeric Arts because they were half an hour from my office and I got on well with the managing director.

But I wanted to increase my profits, and a bold plan started to take shape. What if I developed my own machine? It would need some pretty fancy software, and it would cost a great deal of money to bring it to market.

I wanted to increase my profits, and a bold plan started to take shape. What if I developed my own machine?

I already knew how these machines worked. They plotted an image onto film with a high degree of accuracy. Then the normal photographic process was used to develop the film. Some years earlier, I'd heard about such a machine made by a company called Marconi. Their machine was designed to plot printed circuit boards at high accuracy levels. I thought their machine might work, but it weighed just under one ton—one of the many reasons I couldn't pursue the idea when I worked from my loft in the house! Regardless, I went down to Marconi to see if it really could plot to an accuracy of +/- .005 mms. I was relieved to find that it could.

Now what about the software? I had a business associate

who worked at Synergix, and I knew they wrote good software. I called him one day and invited him for coffee.

"I've always admired your company's software capabilities," I said, "and I wondered if you could write some software that drives a photo plotter to produce very accurate barcode images on film." I was convinced that I'd asked for the impossible.

"Send me a spec," he said, "and I'll give you a quote."

The next day, I faxed over a rough spec of what I wanted, and about a week later the phone rang.

"Hi, Brian," he said. "I've looked at your specification, and we can do it."

I breathed a sigh of relief and then asked the second most important question: "How much will it cost?"

"£50,000," he said.

Oh my God, I thought as my dream quickly died. *How on earth can I afford that much?* I expected it to be around £10,000. £50,000 just wasn't possible.

"Thanks," I said. "I'll get back to you."

I went home that night and brooded about it. I was so excited that they could write the software—which I never thought was possible. But now my raised hopes and dreams were shattered by the enormity of the cost.

I went home to Liz for dinner. I was not good company.

"Cheer up," she said. "You'll think of something. You always do."

And I did. I called him back the next morning.

"I'm really thrilled that you can write this software," I said, "but what if it doesn't work? It's a huge risk for me. I propose that I pay you upon satisfactory completion of the project. Is that acceptable?"

"OK," he said to my huge surprise, shock, and gratitude. "You've got a deal."

We met several times over the next few months as the software took shape. We tweaked it and added things and created a simple user interface. At last, the day of delivery arrived. I'll never forget my feeling of excitement and apprehension as I went to his office to test it out. Would it work?

He sat me in front of a computer, and on the screen appeared the words CINSTEP in four beautiful colors. Then it led me to the input screen, which looked so simple that I managed to create a Film Master immediately. Then I created another, then another, until I had created six. The software automatically found the best fit on the large sheet of film, which meant I could make multiple Film Masters for each plate, thus reducing the unit cost dramatically. It was so brilliant and easy to use.

But it wasn't over yet. I still needed to see if the photo plotter would, in fact, plot these plates to an accuracy of five microns. I took the files to Marconi and downloaded them to their photo plotter. You can imagine my apprehension when they took the plate out of the machine and sent it to the darkroom to develop.

And they were perfect! I was so happy I could sing with joy.

I bought the photoplotter and proudly installed it at Nikon House on the ground floor, which could bear the one-ton weight. We built a darkroom for the film-processing equipment and chemicals, and everything worked like clockwork. My costs went from £5 per Film Master to about £2, and our profits increased accordingly. At its peak, I made about £500,000 profit. Later on, Marconi developed a smaller and cheaper photo plotter, which stood upright and took up very little space. But, in order to run it, our software needed to be modified for the smaller machine. Synergix modified the software and CINSCAN was born! This combination of the smaller photo plotter and modified software was what I later sold in Eastern Europe.

———

As part of my public relations program, *The Daily Telegraph* interviewed me, and they gave the article an entire page. It showed me holding up a sheet of film with Film Masters plotted on it.

The article, of course, was very flattering. It spoke of how I was a bit of a James Bond. They said I'd kept secret the development of a machine that would ultimately lead to my current supplier of Film Masters losing all my business.

My business was pretty important to them and probably accounted for a significant part of their profits. They were a bit shell-shocked when I did, indeed, take all of it away from them overnight. Complacency had set in, and they didn't anticipate that this might happen one day. They offered me a much cheaper price if I would continue working with them, and I wondered why they hadn't offered that price to begin with.

A while after the article was printed, I took a customer to court because they didn't pay their invoice for a desktop printer. There'd been some installation problems, which we had sorted out. The customer hired an attorney to defend him, which I thought was a bit odd since the case was cut and dried—or so I thought. This attorney pulled out *The Daily Telegraph* article and read the James Bond bit out loud. He suggested that this proved I was a shady character, the judge agreed with him, and I lost the case!

———

Unfortunately, my cash cow didn't last forever. In 1992, someone from a label company developed software that produced a barcode straight onto an image setter, which eliminated the need for a Film Master. Produced as an EPS (encapsulated postscript) file that was generated on a PC, the image was sent straight to a design package. The barcode could now be incorporated with the rest of the label's artwork.

The writing was on the wall as more and more people bought the new software when they realized how simple and accurate it was.

The writing was on the wall as more and more people bought the new software when they realized how simple and accurate it was. Then GS1, which is not supposed to compete with their members, started to sell their own EPS files on their website. With that, our market was doomed.

LESSONS LEARNED:

- Nothing lasts forever. Try to anticipate your product's life cycle and look for the signs that a replacement or some kind of market disruption might come along.

- Be resourceful. At the time, it seemed impossible to develop our own software, but when I used my imagination and my network, the dream became a reality. Don't be afraid to ask for help and support.

- Trust people. I trusted Synergix and it paid off.

- Beware of newspaper articles!

QUESTIONS FOR YOU:

- What's on the horizon that could disrupt your marketplace?

- Ask yourself: What business am I really in? What business should I be in?

5 *INCREASE REVENUE*

The barcode—or automatic identification—industry started to grow very fast in the early 80s as more and more products became barcoded. Marketing people and design companies, however, hated the barcode because they thought it spoiled their wonderful label designs. So, they pushed to make the barcode smaller and less intrusive; but the smallest allowable size was 80 percent of the nominal 100 percent (about 30mm x 22mm). If a barcode shrunk any smaller, the scanner couldn't make out the width of the bars and spaces. Even so, reducing the size to 80 percent made it hard for the scanner to read the symbol the first time with such hair's breadth tolerances, and so truncation was born. It was a ploy by the package designers to fit the barcode on a smaller space. If they had their way, the barcode wouldn't exist at all to sully their "glorious" product label designs.

This meant cutting off the tops of the bars, which changed the height/width ratio of the barcode. With this change, a barcode probably wouldn't be scanned the first time unless the checkout person held it at the exact correct angle.

Another challenge that developed involved multiple consumer units that were packed together in corrugated boxes. The corrugation would play havoc with printing the outer case barcode. Pressure from the ink roller would squash the corrugations and smudge the ink. As a result, the scanner would be confused by bars that were wider than it knew how to decode, resulting in scanning errors.

EMERGING MARKETS

This led to the development of a new symbology (barcode type) called ITF-14 (Interleaved 2/5 with 14 digits), which became the new standard for barcoding *cases* of consumer products. The barcode on consumer *units* was called EAN 13, which had thirteen digits. This new symbology included an extra digit. The extra digit at the start was normally a 0, which indicated it was a case code. There followed twelve digits from the EAN 13, with normally just a single digit change in the second half of the code. Then came twelve digits from the consumer unit code. It needed at least one different digit to indicate whether it was a multipack or a consumer unit.

As this new market emerged, we jumped on the opportunity to learn as much technical detail about it as possible. This new technology built on our existing technical knowledge, and we used that to educate our customers and make them feel comfortable that we could help them with everything. In fact, providing an entire solution was our unique selling proposition and was how we built our reputation. We took the mystique out of barcoding and did it better than our competitors. Plus, we had our secret weapon—Judith! Most of the buyers were men, and when a pretty lady entered their office, they preferred to buy from her rather than a smooth-talking guy in a suit!

> *As this new market emerged, we jumped on the opportunity to learn as much technical detail about it as possible.*

As the market grew, we needed to increase revenue. We decided to sell scanners and portable data-capture units, which included a scan engine built into a mobile device with a fair amount of storage in the form of read-only memory (ROM), which is where a program could be stored. For data storage, there was random-access memory (RAM) held in place with an electrical charge.

Now the customer could take a portable data-capture unit—which consisted of a keyboard, screen, and scanner—into a warehouse, count stock, then download the results via a cradle to a computer with their inventory management software on it. The screen gave prompts that told where to go and what to pick, so all they needed to do was scan the bin label under the product, scan the product, and key in how many were picked. This was called *batch process*ing.

Soon Wi-Fi was developed, and some of these devices became equipped with radios, which could access normal Wi-Fi, as well as the GSM mobile phone network. It was now possible to capture data in real time so, for example, instead of scanning goods into stock, you could check if the goods were wanted on the factory floor, which got the right parts in place a couple of days earlier. These new applications gave us new solutions to offer our existing customers.

Our first big sale came at this time with a new device called the wedge: a small box with a light pen scanner attached that sat between the keyboard and the computer. All it did was turn a barcode into data without the need to key in anything. One of our prospects was Red Star Parcels, a railway company. They needed to quickly key enter data from parcels into the computer, so this product was perfect for them.

I pored through my international contacts to see if anyone made a well-priced unit, as the railways are very price sensitive, and I found a US company that signed us up as a distributor. Red Star loved this product, and I went to huge lengths doing pilots and training their staff and configuring the devices to work with their computers. Price, dedication, and enthusiasm delivered the order for us, and it was great for morale.

By the mid 1980s, the barcode industry had grown fast, driven by supermarkets that needed to achieve the magical 80 percent of barcoded stock. The hardware stores were also installing scanners at the till. Because of the nature and shape of their products, an omnidirectional, flatbed scanner favored by supermarkets wouldn't work, so they used hand-held scanners attached to the till. With these, they could reach down if necessary and scan the label on a large, heavy flowerpot on a customer's trolley, for example.

This opened up new markets for self-adhesive barcode labels since it was impossible and undesirable to print a label directly on a flowerpot. Hardware stores stocked all sorts of small items, predominantly in blister packs where it was cheaper to stick a label on the pack rather than print a different barcode for each different type of product. There were also items such as screws that sold in the thousands. You couldn't get a label on them, so what to do? At the checkout, they would scan a menu card with a barcode next to a picture of each type of screw. Of course, other products could be scanned in this way, which created another new market.

Hardware stores stocked other items unsuitable for paper labels, such as rating plates, which needed a barcode printed on metal. Other products needed plastic labels or waterproof labels or rubber labels. This created a whole new industry of printers that could print on these types of materials.

Some of these printers produced blood donor and test tube identification labels for blood banks, which was one of the first nonretail barcode applications. Each blood donor was allocated a set of unique ID labels, and the blood bag containing the donated blood would have a label with the same number. At the laboratory, the blood was put into vials and test tubes for tests such as blood group, red cell antigens, and microbiology. As I write this, the NHS England is about to trial barcodes on medical equipment, hospital assets, and blood bags, with six NHS trusts. They hope that it will save one billion pounds and, of course, lives. This is the first time they've admitted that lives have been lost when the wrong drug or blood type was dispensed.

Some of these printers produced blood donor and test tube identification labels for blood banks, which was one of the first nonretail barcode applications.

It is now twenty-five years since I first spoke to them about barcodes and did trials with blood bags and donor samples. I am very angry about how long this has taken. Now that I don't operate in the UK, I will miss out on all that business!

SUPPLIERS AND TERRITORIES

Our major suppliers of scanners and terminals were Symbol Technology and MSI, who had their own direct sales forces. They wouldn't allow partners such as myself to approach blue-chip companies. This was the exclusive domain of their sales force. This annoyed most Symbol partners, and the sales director of one of them started a dealer association whose purpose it was to interface with Symbol/MSI to pull back from these direct accounts and leave the way clear for us. Needless to say, this was not very successful; but on the positive side, we also got a few concessions as we approached them with a united voice. They didn't want us all to start buying from their competition. Symbol was the most arrogant company I ever dealt with, and a little humility would not have been amiss. In those days, Symbol did not do humility.

This contrasted with our other major supplier, Zebra, the inventor of thermal-transfer printing, the next barcode print revolution. Instead of a print head that heated up and exposed the blue chemicals in the paper to form an image, that same type of print head would melt a plastic ribbon carrying a thin film of ink, which it would transfer onto ordinary label paper to form the image.

At that time, we sold printers from Codeway, Meto, and TEC, a large Japanese company. The sales manager of Esselte Meto was impressive in the way he managed our account, so when he moved to TEC, we followed him and bought his printers instead. When he was asked to form Zebra UK, we started to sell Zebra printers and have never looked back.

Zebra's culture was very different from Symbol's, and I was able to compare the two side by side on one of my visits to the States for the annual Scantech convention, a trade show that featured everything that was happening in the scanning and barcode industry. I was invited to dinner by the top management of both companies on consecutive evenings. First was Symbol, where all the talk was about them and their successes. The second evening was with Zebra, and the conversation was two way and they showed a genuine interest in my company, Bar Code Systems (BCS). Of course, there is no right or wrong in this as both companies are very successful and inventive. Both cultures work, but I think empathy plays a huge role in business as well as in personal life.

On the plus side, Symbol always gave us lots of fun. In the early 1980s when they tried to buy market share, they employed a Dutchman who worked for Plessey, which launched barcodes in the UK. He was another founding member of the barcode industry.

His marketing budget must have been huge, as he would invite all his partners from around the world who visited Scantech in the States for an evening out as Symbol's guests. And it wasn't just any old evening out. One time they reserved a theatre for our exclusive use to hear Ray Charles perform, and another time they took over Universal Studios in Los Angeles for our exclusive use. You can imagine that with no queues I raced around all the rides without a break. This was a great way of marketing, and Symbol became number one, no doubt due in part to this bold initiative.

Around this time, we'd had some ongoing territory disagreements with Symbol, so I thought it was time to seek out markets where there was no conflict with their internal sales force—if that even existed. At that moment, a global earthquake was about to take place: the collapse of the Soviet Union. Mikhail Gorbachev was elected leader of the Russian Politburo in 1985 and embarked upon a policy of *glasnost* (openness) and *perestroika* (restructuring), which appealed to both Margaret Thatcher, then prime minister of the UK, and Ronald Reagan, president of the United States.

> *I thought it was time to seek out markets where there was no conflict with their internal sales force— if that even existed. At that moment, a global earthquake was about to take place: the collapse of the Soviet Union.*

Reagan and Thatcher agreed that Gorbachev was a man they could do business with, and relationships between the three leaders started to thaw. This made me think that Eastern Europe might one day open its borders to the West, the Berlin Wall would be dismantled, and we could march in and do some business.

EXPLORING THE EAST

By now, an association had been formed for those involved in the automatic identification and mobility industry: AIM. I was on the boards of both AIM UK and AIM Europe, and the idea of a Scantech convention in Hungary started to gel. We chose Hungary because Ian Smith, secretary of AIM Europe, was good friends with a doctor who worked for the Hungarian Chamber of Commerce. Smith was going to set up an AIM office in Budapest. There was no Symbol office in Eastern Europe, so it seemed perfect for my next move.

They called the convention Scan Hungary, a small tabletop exhibition. Instead of having a large stand, we had a table and two chairs and put banners behind them explaining what our company offered. At the time, barcode activity in Hungary was on a very small scale, but soon any Hungarian company that wanted to export to the West would have to put barcodes on their products. They would need Film Masters, and I had just the thing for them!

We attracted a lot of curiosity at the exhibition, and soon several people showed an interest in our Film Master machine and software. The plan was to be patient until the Berlin Wall was dismantled—which I hoped would happen—and, in the meantime, to build up some contacts

> **The plan was to be patient until the Berlin Wall was dismantled.**

that I could set up in business there. We repeated Scan Hungary the next year and also opened up Scan Moscow, a very small exhibition with just twelve tables.

Soon after, a contact from the first Scan Hungary, Zdenek Vonasek, came to the UK office to check out the Film Master machine. Zdenek was the one person in Czechoslovakia who knew barcodes. He worked for the state-run printing and publishing company as their barcode expert.

We drove down to Marconi, the manufacturers of my photo plotter. On the way to their offices, I asked him, "Who do you know in Moscow who might be interested in the photo plotter? You said you knew some people in Eastern Europe with similar jobs to your own."

"Yes," he said. "I know Sasha Maximowski from the printing and publishing Computer Centre in Moscow."

"Great," I said. "Let's give him a call."

"What do you mean 'give him a call'—now? How?"

"Sure," I said as I opened up the flap of the armrest and exposed the receiver on my mobile phone, one of the first in the country. "What's his number?"

"You mean you can call Moscow from your car? This is amazing!" gasped Zdenek in disbelief.

So we called Sasha, got introduced, and scheduled an appointment during Scan Moscow.

Zdenek told this story for years after. It must have been a huge culture shock!

After he visited our offices in London, he went back to Prague and placed an order for my Film Master machine. Since it couldn't go through his company, it was purchased through the state company that was licensed to trade with Western companies, and an allocation of foreign currency was granted to them for this purpose.

This brings us to 1989 and the fall of the Berlin Wall.

LESSONS LEARNED:

- Learn to deal with different cultures. You'll find that many people won't know your culture and values, but you need to find ways to adapt and deal with them. Do not impose your culture on them but find ways to coexist without conflict. You can soon adopt the best of both cultures and learn from each other.

- Don't stay in your own limited world. Think big and have a big vision, and if outside forces prevent you from getting where you want to be, think of ways to overcome them. Seize the opportunity when it comes; and if it doesn't come, find one yourself. Opportunities do not come often, so you can't afford to let one pass you by. Be brave. What is the worst that can happen, and does it matter? Seek out new markets and go where others haven't been before you. That way you can set the agenda that others will have to follow.

QUESTIONS FOR YOU:

- Have you ever said to yourself, "What's the worst that can happen if I do such and such?" Did you do it? Did it work?

- If you didn't do it, why not? What would you have done differently?

- Do you consider yourself to be brave?

6 *LOOK FOR NEW MARKETS*

I t was a huge thrill to land in Budapest for the first Scan Hungary; there was such a sense of adventure. After all, nobody from our industry had set foot there before.

I was happy to be on British Airways, which flew direct from London to Budapest once per day. Malev, the Hungarian airline, flew Russian planes such as the Tupolev 54, which was Russia's answer to the Boeing 727. That aircraft didn't, however, have the best reputation for safety. I once flew in one on a flight from Budapest to Prague. It was very old fashioned: threadbare carpets, loose seats that weren't bolted to the floor, and very dim cabin lights. The air hostesses could not be bothered about safety briefings, and we heard no announcements from the pilot the entire flight. Although it was only a forty-minute flight, I was terrified throughout. It was several years before you could fly between Budapest and Prague on a Boeing.

Budapest was the first place I set foot in Eastern Europe. The terminal was austere. It was like a huge concrete block, and there were long queues at immigration where they checked our visas.

As we entered Budapest, I expected to see characterless Slavonic concrete buildings, but I was delighted to see some beautiful architecture. There was a mixture of Baroque and Renaissance buildings and some churches in Gothic style. Heroes Square is a beautiful place noted for its iconic statue complex, which features the Seven Chieftains of the Magyars and other important national leaders, as well as the Tomb of the Unknown Soldier. Other buildings were similar to those in Vienna, like the Opera, which were reminders of the Austro-Hungarian Empire.

Budapest joins two formerly separate cities—Buda and Pest—that are divided by the River Danube. Buda is on one bank and Pest is on the other. I stayed on the Pest side at the Intercontinental Hotel, which was the only decent Western-style hotel at the time. It had a beautiful position on the Danube with glorious views over to Buda and the Castle District, as well as the Matthias Church with its beautiful red and green roof, accessible via the iconic Elisabeth Bridge (Erzsébet híd).

It was best to avoid the local hotels. Although cheap, the food was horrible, and the beds were narrow with thin mattresses, a light duvet cover, and a thin pillow. To this day, local bedrooms in most Eastern European countries are similar.

In those days I used to run marathons, so I got up around 7:00 a.m. and ran along the river front, past the Houses of Parliament onto Margaret Island, down to the end, back up the other side of the river, across the bridge, and back to the hotel. All in all, it was about five kilometers. The route had spectacular views and, apart from the hazards of the tramlines, it was quite safe from traffic.

The biggest thrill was my first visit to Moscow in 1988. Because it was during the Cold War, it was like eating forbidden fruit.

Visiting Budapest for the first time was a thrill; however, the biggest thrill was my first visit to Moscow in 1988. Because it was during the Cold War, it was like eating forbidden fruit. It was behind the Iron Curtain, which is actually just a metaphor. However, when in Moscow, you could almost see and feel it. The days were dominated by low, heavy grey clouds that made it very oppressive.

MOSCOW

It was always a performance to visit Moscow because I had to obtain a visa, which cost £100 and involved a visit to the Russian embassy in London. Anything having to do with Russia involves incredibly long lines and interminable waits. There were always enormous queues at the embassy, at the end of which I had to hand over my passport. Some days later, I would return to queue up again to pick up my passport and visa.

To get there, good old British Airways came to the rescue with Boeing 767s and an occasional 747 for the three-hour flight, which cost £900! Those were the days when my travel bill exceeded £25,000 per year compared to about £3,000 now. What a wonderful thing market forces are!

We landed at Sheremetyevo International Airport, eighteen miles north of Moscow. The airport was dark; electricity was used sparingly, and fluorescent lights were not yet available. What struck me was the bleakness of it all. No advertising to brighten the concrete walls, and the air was thick with pungent cigarette smoke. Cigarettes were very cheap, and most Eastern Bloc people smoked a great deal.

More waiting. The queues at immigration were legendary. Everyone was scrutinized as they passed through, and there was no order in the lines. People just crowded around the desks as they waited their turn. It took at least an hour. I was quite apprehensive about whether my visa would be accepted or if the KGB would detain me. Not a rational thought, I know, but these things went through my mind, probably due to too much exposure to spy films.

Once through the airport, we started on the long journey to Moscow. It took about an hour and a half. The traffic was horrible, and the intersections hadn't been properly designed, which led to many jams.

Moscow's main streets were unexpectedly wide and had several lanes, but the buildings were bleak. Stalin had been influential in designing the buildings, and he created seven tower blocks known as wedding cakes, or the Seven Sisters, a term not familiar to Muscovites, who call them Stalin's high-rises or Stalin's skyscrapers. They were located at strategic points in a ring to reflect the radial layout of the city. Stalin built these because he'd been concerned that Westerners would one day visit Moscow and wonder why there were no skyscrapers, unlike most famous Western cities, which would be humiliating to Russia.

The seven buildings are Hotel Ukraina, Moscow State University, the Ministry of Foreign Affairs, the Leninsgradksaya Hotel, the Kotelnicheskaya Embankment Building, the Kudrinskaya Square Building, and the Red Gates Administrative Building. The buildings are characterized by large, stout bases and a sweeping crown. At the peak of each is a central spire, which was added as an afterthought to compete with US skyscrapers.

The shops were all monochromatic and looked exactly alike. They had no names, just numbers. For example, you visited pharmacy number fifty-eight or butcher number twenty-three and so on. And, because of communism, there wasn't much on the shelves. It was a planned economy where goods and food got allocated to regions based on a five- or ten-year plan. The state controlled all the assets and fixed the prices, which had no bearing on value at all.

In fact, the custom was to barter or exchange, say, one sheep for ten loaves of bread or many variants on that theme. Currency was used only for accounting purposes. Thus, there were infernal queues for everything, as demand always outstripped supply. With no foreign currency to buy Western products and a ban on travel to the West, unless you had a travel permit, the quality of goods never improved. In fact, to this day Russia doesn't produce high-quality products that are world leaders in innovation.

At the present moment, the leaders of Russia are trying to modernize but, unfortunately, like their predecessors, they try to separate technology from socio-political systems by suppressing political opponents and entrepreneurs. They twist the legal system to serve their own ends, they sign laws that threaten Russians who work with foreigners with treason, and they create a regressive authoritarian regime. Such policies do not lead to a society with risk-taking entrepreneurs and rebellious innovators.

On the plus side, Red Square was fabulous. Upon entering it, my first impression was one of huge majesty. You enter through a gate, which opens out into a huge cobbled square—though not a square as we know it but a long rectangle which has the capacity to hold the whole of Russia's military might.

On the left was Gum, Russia's attempt at a shopping mall. Again, each shop had no name but a number and was stocked with a reasonable variety of goods not usually available. Fast-forward to present time, and Gum houses very fashionable clothing shops from Western designers with the price tags to match. What a transformation! Barcodes and scanning tills are in every shop, and it feels like you could be anywhere in the world.

Opposite the gate is St. Basil's Cathedral, officially known as the Cathedral of the Intercession of the Virgin by the Moat. It's actually eight churches that are built around a ninth. It looks like colored onions on top of a wide cake base and is so beautiful. No services are held there anymore because it's now a museum.

The Kremlin flanks the right side and houses Lenin's Tomb, which sees a steady procession of pilgrims as they file past. Behind the cathedral, there used to be a hideous international hotel with three thousand rooms called the Rossiya, which was demolished in 2006.

On January 30, 1990, the first McDonald's restaurant opened in Moscow—the first in the Soviet Union. It's said that McDonald's held talks with Soviet officials about opening the venture for over twenty years. Similar to my deals with the joint ventures, McDonald's offered 51 percent ownership to the Soviet state. On the first day, they expected one thousand people but, in fact, thirty thousand people arrived. This shows just how deprived the Soviets were of even a good restaurant. The price of a Big Mac soon became the indicator for Eastern European economies as McDonald's expanded into the other Eastern Bloc countries, where they set prices based on the average monthly salaries.

> **The beginning of the end of the Iron Curtain was on May 2, 1989, when Hungary dismantled its 150-mile wall with Austria.**

The beginning of the end of the Iron Curtain was on May 2, 1989, when Hungary dismantled its 150-mile wall with Austria, which allowed many East Germans on holiday there to cross over into West Germany and freedom. Gorbachev did nothing in response.

EXPANSION TO THE EAST

My grand plan was to make contacts at the Scan Hungary and Scan Moscow exhibitions, in hopes that I could find some people with an entrepreneurial bent who might want to set up a joint venture. I would have to finance these joint ventures (JVs) so that there was some working capital.

At that time, the banking system was not transparent, and it wasn't possible to borrow money, especially from an English bank that didn't understand Eastern Europe at all. They were very wary of Eastern Europe, and we all know how much banks hate risks. My plan was to sell one Film Master machine and the software in each country at about £25,000 profit. It would be purchased and run by the state and would create some working capital for the JVs. All I needed to do was find these entrepreneurial people and decide how to split the shares with them.

After the Wall came down, the Eastern Bloc countries had to deal with multiple Western countries instead of just Russia. They also needed to learn the word *sell*. In their planned economy, there was no such word. Consumers simply bought what the state told them to in whatever quantities and at whatever price it dictated.

Most state-owned heavy industries were privatized through the voucher privatization system. Under this system, every citizen was given the opportunity to buy, for a moderate price, a book of vouchers that represented shares in any state-owned company. The voucher holders could then invest their vouchers, which increased the capital base of the chosen company and created a nation of citizen shareholders. This is in contrast to Russian privatization, where they sold communal assets to private companies rather than transfer shares to citizens.

The effect of this policy has been dramatic. Under communism, state ownership of businesses in Russia was estimated to be 97 percent. Privatization through restitution of real estate to the former owners was largely completed in 1992. Six years later, more than 80 percent of enterprises were in private hands.

JOINT VENTURES

My first major contact from Scan Hungary was Zdenek Vonasek, who worked at the Czechoslovakian printing company. I liked him a lot and so he became my first partner. He spoke English well and understood printing and barcodes, but he worked for a state company and wasn't allowed to leave that position. So what to do? Two colleagues worked with Zdenek in his department, and if I could take the three of them, I knew we could start a great little business together.

I suddenly had a brainwave about how to do it. I made an appointment with Zdenek's boss, a nasty little man called Herr Schneider who was in a dead-end job and would never adapt to a free-market economy.

At 9:00 a.m. I knocked on his office door.

"Come in," said a surly voice in Czech. Thick with smoke, I entered a small office with faded photos of Stalin on the walls that were otherwise bare. Herr Schneider sat behind an ancient small, wooden office desk and waved me to the only chair in the room. It was so small and uncomfortable that I couldn't wait to get out.

"Herr Schneider," I said to him in my best German, "I would like to buy the services of Zdenek Vonasek and the other two employees. I will give you $1000 if you let them leave your company tomorrow."

To my huge surprise and delight—and to some extent expectation, as corruption was rife at the time—he agreed. But only if I paid him cash.

I was prepared. I handed over $1000 in cash, which represented about six months of salary for him. I expect it didn't get further than his own pocket.

Afterward, we were all very excited to start our first joint venture. However, I needed to form a company to do this, and private citizens couldn't start companies in Eastern Europe. So in 1990, I founded International Bar Code Systems (IBCS) as a holding company.

Next, I needed to work out a structure for the joint venture: what sort of shares to offer, whether I should charge for them, what would be the roles and responsibilities of each party, what would *my* role even be since I didn't speak the language and couldn't possibly spend a lot of time in Prague.

That's when the culture of the partners-to-be was born. Since my partners weren't investing their own money and we didn't have a bank loan, we decided to use the profits from the Film Master machine to raise capital. I decided to give Zdenek 51 percent of the shares and kept 49 percent for myself.

"You mean you gave up control," I hear you cry, "to someone you didn't know in a country that you didn't know in a market you didn't know—and you gave them £25,000 to play with?"

Yes, I did! I figured this was the only way to finance the business and to motivate Zdenek. It was crucial that he owned the business, so it was like his baby. If he wanted to, he could cut me out and move the assets into another company or do some crooked deal. But he could do that whether I had 100 percent or 49 percent, so why not give the control to him to demonstrate trust and give him ownership?

I figured this was the only way to finance the business and to motivate Zdenek. It was crucial that he owned the business, so it was like his baby.

To this day, I feel these are the two greatest gifts I could have given him, and as a result, business has boomed. The loyalty was cemented, and the IBCS culture and joint-venture model were born.

We needed to call ourselves something, and Bar Code Systems or even BCS didn't work in Czech. So Zdenek came up with the name Kodys. We figured we would need about 850 square feet for an office. It was the equivalent of about three rooms, and instead of an office building, Zdenek decided to move into a shop! I disagreed with this idea until he explained his reasons. He felt that since we would be printing self-adhesive barcode labels to stick on products slated for export to the West, we should display them in the window to attract passers-by.

I thought that was ridiculous. Who would be attracted to a shop that sold barcodes? But Zdenek convinced me, and that day I learned he was an independent thinker, a quality which often challenged my own strategic thought processes. I was secretly pleased that he would not be a yes-man. He was right about renting the shop, of course, and we started to do great business.

INTO RUSSIA

Meanwhile, my contacts in Moscow through Scan Moscow started to bear fruit. I had met with Sasha Maximowski, the man who took the surprise mobile call the previous year, and he expressed an interest in starting a joint venture because he needed to produce barcodes for books. He was the computer expert for the state printing and publishing company in Russia, similar to the one in Prague whom Zdenek represented, and they knew each other.

As you can imagine, in 1990 Russians looked for any excuse to travel to the West where they could stock up on cameras, records, and all sorts of decadent goods like *Playboy* magazine, which they either kept or sold on their return to Moscow. Sasha's boss and a couple of his colleagues persuaded their bosses that they needed to visit London to check out the Film Master machine. They made several visits and brought a copious supply of foreign currency with them. After each visit, they would return to Moscow laden with goods.

These visits were expensive for me. They needed accommodations in the local pub, to be taken out for meals, and—since they didn't speak English—an interpreter. I hired the best interpreter I could find; her claim to fame was that she had interpreted for Gorbachev on his visit to London. And she was a looker, too—just as well for her price tag of £200 per day!

> **The cost of the interpreter was a heavy expense, and the only way to avoid it was to learn Russian myself.**

The cost of the interpreter was a heavy expense, and the only way to avoid it was to learn Russian myself. I was quite good in languages and had studied French, German, and Italian at school. So, I hired a middle-aged Russian lawyer to teach me the language, and he came to my house for a one-on-one lesson every week. I loved the Russian characters, the Cyrillic script, and very much enjoyed reading and writing the language. But the teacher didn't do much oral work, so my fluency was poor even after four years of lessons.

You can imagine my huge surprise when Sasha came to England on his own four months after we'd met in Moscow, when he didn't speak a word of English. And he was now fluent!

How could this be? He'd gone to an English tutor every day for that four months. Such dedication and commitment were so impressive.

Anyway, I carried on learning Russian, as it is a rather beautiful language. Some of the words are similar to Polish, Czech, and Slovakian and, of course, Bulgarian, so it comes in useful sometimes to pick up the odd word.

We did have fun together on those visits. One time, we all went to the Little Angel pub just outside Henley for lunch. It was May 9—Victory Day in Russia—an important military milestone in Russian history when the Soviet army marched triumphantly into Berlin in 1945. My guests rightfully needed to celebrate, and their way of doing so was to take a shot of vodka while standing at attention and singing rousing Russian songs. Once was not enough, so it happened six times. Of course, they became louder each time, as the drink worked its magic. This amused the clientele, and the pub soon ran out of vodka.

———

Of course, I also visited Moscow to check on our business. Moscovites liked to impress their guests by showing that they could get things others in the "proletariat" could not. So when they entertained, they started with enormous amounts of food—hors d'oeuvres, then platefuls of different types of fish. Then came the meat, followed by ice cream with chocolate sauce. Their hospitality knew no bounds, and I enjoyed many an abundant meal in Sasha's flat with his gorgeous wife, Lena, and his daughters, Mariana and Jana.

One night, after another great meal provided by Lena, we left their flat, which was several kilometers outside Moscow Centre. I asked Sasha how I would get back to the hotel. It was so late, and he was not fit to drive.

"Don't worry," he said. "Come with me."

We went down the tiny lift and emerged on the street to a blast from a bitterly cold wind. It must have been -20 Celsius, which is -4 Fahrenheit. We fought the wind and snow as we made our way to the main road. Sasha put up his right thumb as if to hail a taxi.

Before long, a car pulled up and Sasha chatted at length with the driver, opened the back door of the car, and beckoned for me to get in.

"Sasha, this is not a taxi," I protested.

"Don't worry," he said. "I have paid him, and he will take you to the hotel."

"What if I get kidnapped?" I asked.

"Don't worry," he said. "Nothing will happen to you."

Quite uneasy, I got in the car and settled back for the long drive. I wondered why this chap was driving me back to the hotel and why he'd been cruising the streets this late at night. *Where were the taxis?* I thought.

I arrived at the hotel in one piece and found out that there was such high unemployment and such low wages in Russia that private car owners would take you anywhere to earn some cash. The precursor to Uber, I suspect!

THE UNDERSIDE OF BUSINESS

In 1990, the Russians bought two Film Master machines and some laser verifiers for £160,000. We were now in business in Moscow with Sasha our designated partner, although it was actually the state printing and publishing company, which couldn't be seen doing direct business with a Westerner. Our office was in their building, and we could use their facilities. We called ourselves Inter Bar Code, because every business involved with foreigners included *In* or *Inter* in its name.

It was so exciting to have a JV in Russia, and we were trailblazers—only the ninth foreign registered JV. I was most excited about this JV because Russia was the Cold War personified and was full of spies and the KGB. It was also a huge challenge to do business there because the state owned the banks, and only one or two were allowed to trade in foreign currency. There was no free-market economy, and there was so much corruption. We had to keep three sets of books: one real set that was kept under the table and two for the police who came to audit. They would want a bribe, based on their interpretation of the law. The auditors would define the laws in three different ways, and we chose the set of accounts that matched the auditor's definition of the law at the time, for which he demanded a $50,000 bribe.

To try to beat, or even play, the system took a very skillful player, and Sasha was an absolute master. In fact, he spent more time trying to beat the system than growing the business! However, this enabled us to survive for over five years.

The audit process was unnerving. One time, some men with guns came into our Moscow office unannounced. They told us to go in the back room while they looked through our books.

"They're from the mafia," Sasha said. "We call them *bratki*, or mobsters. We must do as they say. I've been fighting them for three months with help from a Special Forces friend from the Army. They want to sell me a "roof," which is someone whom we have to pay to protect our business. Let's see what they do."

I was terrified. I followed Sasha into the back room where we waited for several hours. We could hear them pulling out drawers and moving things around in our stock room. After about six hours, one of them came in to see Sasha and mumbled something in Russian.

"They haven't found anything," he said in a low voice. "In fact, they're going away now. They said there's no money in barcodes, so they aren't going to waste any more of their time."

The mobsters trooped out of the office and banged the door shut.

Another time I got a phone call from Sasha, who sounded in a panic.

"Brian, we must take our money out of our bank immediately. I have a tip that the bank is about to steal our money! I will fax something for you to sign, so please sign it right away!"

How is this possible? I thought. *Surely the banks are safe.* But no, they were not. In fact, today they're still quite shaky because there's no transparency. I received the fax, signed and returned it immediately. Later, Sasha said he got the money out with only thirty minutes to spare!

But it wasn't all cloak-and-dagger dealings in Russia. In fact, some of their policies worked in our favor. It was decreed that all bottles of alcohol must have a paper stamp with a barcode applied to the neck of the bottle, which would bring revenue to the taxman. Sasha estimated this could be worth between eighty million dollars and one hundred million dollars per year to us.

We sold millions of these labels until, one day, Sasha was summoned to the customer location. It turned out that the business was run by a KGB representative, and he told Sasha that they planned to take over our business. Sasha tried to fight it, but he was threatened by a lieutenant general from the KGB, who said they would kill his family unless he stopped the business.

And that was the end of that.

LESSONS LEARNED:

- Listen to others and don't be dogmatic. You're not the only one who has great ideas. When you adopt other people's ideas, it empowers them and encourages them to be even more inventive. If you shut them down, you'll develop a culture that lacks innovation, which will demotivate your staff.

- For the same reason, don't surround yourself with yes-men. You need to be challenged because, as a company owner, you need to be able to bounce ideas off someone. You don't want people who agree with you all the time.

- Try to enjoy life's rich experiences, like being held at gunpoint and even maybe kidnapped by a random car driver!

QUESTIONS FOR YOU:

- Think of a time when someone came to you with a great idea. Did you take it on, pat him on the back, and give him the credit? Or did you ignore it because it came from a staff member you didn't much like?

- Have you hired people who are better than you at any level? Why do you think it's important?

7 WHEN BUSINESS TURNED PERSONAL

In 1990, Iraq invaded Kuwait, which led to the first Gulf War. It was Iraq against the United States and thirty-four nations in defense of Saudi Arabia, which in turn led to the combat phase called Operation Desert Storm the following year. The consequences of this were to have a profound effect on my life.

During that conflict, many wounded soldiers died on the battlefield because they received the wrong blood type when transfused. The blood bags were poorly labeled in many different languages. Different blood types were printed in different colors, but they couldn't be read by many of the medics because they were color blind.

To avoid a repeat of this, some years later blood bag labels had to be printed in black, which paved the way for the label to be produced by a thermal-transfer printer, which of course we sold! This was to change the whole blood-transfusion industry, and it offered our company a great new marketplace, which I embraced.

RAISE THE BAR

Later that year, Dr. Wang at Symbol Technologies invented a new symbology called PDF 417. This was the first two-dimensional symbology—or barcode—with the bars and spaces stacked one on top of the other, like a skyscraper. The height of the bars was reduced to create space. This fostered a change in the industry because the data had always been contained within the width of the bars, not the height. Now both were at play.

It was called PDF, or portable data file, and it contained up to one kilobyte of data that could represent anything digitizable, such as a signature, photograph, or standard alphanumerics. Unlike a one-dimensional barcode, which is simply a key that references a database of prices and product description, PDF carried the database *with* it, so all that data was available offline. It was called 417 because each pattern in the code consisted of four bars and spaces and was seventeen units long.

It was an incredible symbology because it used different densities based on the amount of security put in the symbol, so at maximum security, half the code could be destroyed yet could still be read due to data redundancy—data repeated throughout the symbol. Furthermore, a laser scanner with multiple scan beams that oscillated up and down the symbol could read it.

> *I was really excited about this revolution and started to picture all sorts of applications—like driver licenses and identity cards for a start—but it also occurred to me that it would be perfect for blood bags.*

I was really excited about this revolution and started to picture all sorts of applications—like driver licenses and identity cards for a start—but it also occurred to me that it would be perfect for blood bags. A blood bag needed seven different types of labels attached to it for the blood type, donor identification number, and various test results. With PDF 417, they could all be represented in just one barcode.

In 1993, I started trials with the Oxford Regional Blood Transfusion Centre at John Radcliffe Hospital, where director Dr. Marlene Fisher shared my vision to replace these disparate barcode labels with one PDF 417 barcode and print the whole label using the thermal-transfer printer. In addition, the system would capture all the different donation numbers in each box of blood and put them into a PDF symbol so that in one scan, a whole box of blood bags could be received into the database of the transfusion center.

As a result of Desert Storm, the International Society of Blood Transfusion formed a group called WPADP (Working Party on Automation and Data Processing) to develop and implement a new international standard based on a new symbology called Code 128. Up until then, barcodes could encode only a limited number of alphanumeric characters in one code, depending on the width of the scanner beam. But with Code 128, all ASCII characters could be encoded, and it was much denser.

I joined this working party as the barcode expert and helped with its development. Blood transfusion became a major focus of mine, and I was determined to wake the Department of Health up to the substantial number of fatalities caused by the wrong blood type given to the soldiers. My successful crusade started in 1993, when I called on our National Blood Transfusion Service to implement the standard in the UK, but only recently have the hospitals woken up to the benefits to the National Health Service. I didn't know how personal it would get.

———

Liz and I couldn't have children due to a large, benign growth in her stomach, which left adhesions on her fallopian tubes when it was removed. IVF didn't work, as it was in its infancy and very expensive. We agreed that we wouldn't adopt any children. We were both too old to be allowed to adopt any but a disabled child, and with the demands of our business, we would be unable to cope.

Around October 1990, Channel 4 broadcast a program called "Ceausescu's Children," a documentary about orphanages in Romania. They told how Nicolae Ceausescu, the president of Romania, wanted to grow a super state and had passed a decree in 1966 that banned abortion unless a family already had four children. He hoped this would lead to economic growth. As a result, there was an increase in the number of births, and many children were abandoned in orphanages that were also occupied by people with disabilities and mental illnesses. Together, these vulnerable groups were subjected to institutionalized neglect, physical and sexual abuse, and medications to control their behavior.

Orphanages lacked both medicines and washing facilities. The children were often tied to their own beds and restrained in their own clothes. Physical and sexual abuse was reported to be common, and the children often spent their day naked because the staff failed to put clothes on them. They sat in their own urine.

Nurses worked at the institutions with no proper training and often abused the children. They bathed them in dirty bath water, thrown in three at a time by the workers. Due to the abuse children received from staff, the older ones learned to beat the younger ones. The staff shaved all their heads, which made it difficult to differentiate which child was which. This led to delayed cognitive development, and many children had no idea how to feed themselves. Physical needs were not met, and many children died from minor illness or injuries, such as cataracts or anemia. Some also starved to death. Physical injuries included fractures that didn't heal properly, resulting in deformed limbs. Unsterilized instruments infected kids with HIV/AIDS. Overall, the orphanages failed to meet even the most basic needs of the children.

Liz was deeply moved by the plight of these children and wanted to go to Romania to volunteer in the orphanages for a few weeks. She wrote to Channel 4 and offered her services, but they said she didn't have the skills needed.

"Ceausescu's Children" followed on from a TV program that featured Anneka Rice, a famous broadcaster. She was challenged to take some volunteers to an orphanage in Romania and completely refurbish it, sanitize it, and bring joy and presents to the children—all of which was meant to give their plight a great deal of publicity. Their stories also moved a great number of foreigners to go to Romania and adopt children of various ages. In fact, Romania was the most popular country for people seeking to adopt children in the late 1980s.

On December 1, 1990, I was watching one of my godchildren play rugby while Liz went off to a seminar about Romania that was organized by a friend who happened to be the son of the leader of the People's Party of Romania, an opposition party. When she came to pick me up, her first words were, "We're going to adopt a Romanian baby."

> **When she came to pick me up, her first words were, "We're going to adopt a Romanian baby."**

"OK," I said without another thought. I'd also been moved by their plight.

There followed a grueling six months during which we got assigned a social worker who would report on whether we were suitable to adopt a child.

In April 1991, we found out that we passed the tests, so we booked travel to Romania in search of a child. My fabulous Czech partner, Zdenek, volunteered to drive us there in his Skoda. He knew an ex-member of the Romanian Red Cross who lived in Prague, and he offered to use his contacts in the Red Cross to visit the orphanages, so we wouldn't have to go through official channels. If we had used the official channels, we would have had to apply to the Romanian authorities, who would have simply allocated a child to us. We'd heard horror stories, mainly from Americans, who'd gone to see their assigned child for the first time. In some cases, there was no child, so they lost their money. In other cases, the child was missing a limb or had some other disability. One thing was certain: there was no choice but to take the child offered.

Zdenek agreed to collect Liz and me from Budapest Hungary, the nearest country to Romania. He drove a blue Skoda, and I wondered how Liz and I would last the several days of traveling in the back seat. There was not much room to move around. Also, the roads through Hungary were pretty rough.

We reached the border of Romania at Szeged, where we joined a long line of cars that wanted to make the crossing. The border guards took an age to check everybody's passport, but we finally got through. The first big town we entered was Oradea, and we got to work visiting the orphanages there.

It was exactly as depicted on the television program. Wrought iron beds were pushed close together, each one holding a small child who lay in their own urine. Their eyes were huge, but they stared blankly into space. We saw few nurses, none of whom gave one-on-one attention to stimulate these kids, who were left to their own devices. They were rail thin and some were completely naked. The stench was almost overpowering. You could cut the despair in the atmosphere with a knife, and all I wanted to do was escape as quickly as possible.

We travelled south to the next big town of Arad. Here, I started to think about the HIV and hepatitis B viruses that were prevalent in most of the children. I caught sight of the blood bags they used. Because they were so malnourished, the children all needed blood transfusions. Unsterilized needles were reused from child to child, which is how the diseases were transmitted. There were no barcodes, of course, and the labels were stenciled, not printed, and in different colors to depict each blood group.

Because they were so malnourished, the children all needed blood transfusions. Unsterilized needles were reused from child to child, which is how the diseases were transmitted.

I was told that Arad, Oradea, and Timisoara (the capital of western Romania) formed a common blood transfusion area, so I hatched a plan. I called my friend Terry Dunn, whose company printed blood labels, to see if he would like to help prevent the spread of these diseases and make the blood tracking more efficient. He immediately agreed to donate one million blood labels with barcodes. I donated the scanning equipment along with Symbol Technologies.

We spent about five nights in ghastly hotels. The locals stole the light bulbs, so we were often left in darkness or semidarkness. I knew the food would be bad, and we'd brought a stock of biscuits and other favorites when we left England, so we had some nice comfort food to keep us going.

At an orphanage in Arad, Liz saw a little two-year-old girl and decided that she wanted to adopt her. But to get approval for the adoption from the Home Office in the United Kingdom, the girl needed to be clear of HIV and hepatitis B, so we had to get her blood tested. The nearest laboratory was in Bucharest. It was at least six hundred kilometers away (almost 375 miles), and there was no airport nearby. And we had no car. The only way to get there was by train, which turned out to be an overnight journey—a ten-hour train journey. Fortunately, the train had bunks, which were dimly lit and very depressing. It seemed to crawl along and rattled all the way. It was very difficult to get a good night's sleep.

We arrived at 7:00 a.m. on a Saturday. Problem was that the lab was shut on weekends, but because of my involvement with barcodes and blood transfusion, they said they would stay open and have the results for us on Monday. Meanwhile, we stayed at the sole Western hotel in Bucharest—the Intercontinental—which was packed full of American women waiting for their embassy to grant a visa to the child they hoped to adopt, which in some cases took up to two months. This was where we heard all the harrowing stories, and they didn't fill us with encouragement.

Monday delivered the worst news. The girl was both HIV and hepatitis B positive, so there was no way we could take her back to the UK. Liz was distraught and by now we must have seen about four hundred children in various orphanages. Soon our visa would run out. We didn't have time to visit a whole lot more orphanages, so what to do?

The previous week on our visit to Resitá not far from Timisoara, we had found a lovely lawyer who agreed to handle any legality when and if we found a child. Her name was Adrianna. She didn't speak English but did speak French, so that's the language we conversed in. I told her that the child we wanted to adopt was ill, and she said she'd look around Resitá for a child while we stayed in Bucharest. A couple of days went by with no news from her. She finally called and said she'd found three possible children, but only one seemed suitable. She was a preemie—just born—and was in hospital in an incubator. Her mother planned to place her in an orphanage when she recovered. The woman already had a five-year-old and couldn't afford another child. Would we like to see the child?

It was a gamble, but our visa would soon run out. This was our last chance.

We took the overnight train back to Resitá and went to the hospital with Adrianna to meet the mother. The tiny little week-old baby was wrapped so tightly in a white towel that we could see only her little red nose, eyes, and forehead. We both fell in love with her instantly. Yes, we would adopt her if the mother gave her permission, which she did. But first we needed to test her for HIV/hep B as usual, so they needed to give us her blood. They took her away to a back room, but we could still hear her screams as the doctor stuck a needle in her head. He assured us that this was how to take blood from a baby.

Off we went back to Bucharest that night. We took the blood to the lab the next day and, joy of joys, she was clear. Back on the train, we returned to Resitá to meet the family and prepare the paperwork.

While we went to Bucharest, we left Jess at the hospital in Resitá. I left explicit instructions not to give her a transfusion, so she wouldn't get infected. I knew she needed one; she weighed less than two pounds. To my horror, they did transfuse her, so I asked the doctor for the blood-bag number. I got my friend at the lab in Bucharest to track the donor of the blood. We found out that she was clear of disease, and we brought our daughter home.

8 *NEED ACCESS TO CAPITAL*

I n the beginning, there was no need to borrow money for the business because we had tight control of our cash, low overhead with a home office, just two of us in the company, and the cost of our raw materials was low. In our first year, we turned over £72,000 and made a net profit of £14,000, of which we were very proud!

Entrepreneurs have to be risk takers—and that means with their own money. In most cases, startups don't need to borrow money unless they have expensive equipment or a large amount of stock. But as your business grows, you'll need access to capital so you can put items into stock and quickly serve your customers.

> **Entrepreneurs have to be risk takers. And that means with their own money.**

The cheapest form of financing, other than a mortgage, is a bank overdraft, or line of credit. You could consider remortgaging your house if there's been growth in the market price, but you have to remember that if the business fails, you can lose it. A bank overdraft is another option, but it comes with the dreaded personal guarantee, which simply means that you guarantee repayment of the loan with your personal assets. If you can't repay the overdraft, you could still lose your house. Some banks will lend you £10,000 without a personal guarantee, but you might need more money than that.

BOOM TO BANKRUPT

The hard truth is that revenue and profits are important, but cash is king. You have to keep constant watch on your cash flow. Allow me to explain.

In 2000, I owned two companies: Bar Code Systems (BCS) for UK business and International Bar Code Systems (IBCS), which purchased product from our suppliers and resold it at a 15 percent margin to our partners in Eastern Europe. The high margin was to cover our finance costs and risks, as well to pay for my services to the partners.

One day an opportunity presented itself. A company called Axis wanted to sell their Film Master business. They asked £50,000 for it, and since they had a strong customer base, it was obvious that the payback would be only one year. The plan was for their customers to transfer to our supply chain at no extra cost. A no-brainer, I thought.

Armed with this very simple business plan, I went to the bank and asked to borrow £50,000 as a loan or as an increase in overdraft. Instead of loaning me the money, our bank relationship manager put us into incubation! The bank blocked our account, and any money that came in from debtors was taken from our account to repay the overdraft. We had to ask for permission to pay any of our creditors, but at least the bank allowed us to pay the staff.

How could such a cast-iron business proposition turn into a journey to insolvency?

How could such a cast-iron business proposition turn into a journey to insolvency?

"What happened?" you ask. "How could those bankers be so idiotic?" Just what I thought.

Here's what happened: the bank's software programs had algorithms that did a sanitary check on Bar Code Systems and projected our cash flow over the next twelve months. The report showed that we would run out of cash by the end of the period. That was an incredible projection and was, indeed, exactly what came to pass. They saw that the Eastern Europe business was growing so fast that it would need more and more cash to fund the extra turnover, and they weren't prepared to finance that expansion.

With this turn of events, we had to manage our creditors. We called each one and asked if they would grant us extra time to pay. We were in the UK, so our creditors included the VAT and Inland Revenue, which both put us on a payment plan. In addition, we had to try to get our debtors to pay us early. We didn't want to raise any suspicions, so we had to handle these conversations very carefully. Meanwhile, our Russian joint venture defaulted on £60,000 because one of the customers went bust, and some other Eastern European debtors extended their payment times. The writing was on the wall. We felt doomed. Or were we?

A friend put me in touch with a company that specialized in situations like ours. They suggested we applied for a CVA, or company voluntary arrangement, whereby the company enters into a legally binding agreement with its creditors. Payments to them are frozen while the company works to trade out of its problems. A licensed insolvency practitioner is appointed, and he makes sure both sides stick to the agreement—a bit like Chapter 11 bankruptcy in the States, I suppose.

We owed our two main suppliers, Symbol and Zebra, in excess of £250,000 each. I visited each of them and told them they'd never get paid and that, in fact, we had applied for a CVA. If they would write off the debt, we could continue to trade in another guise when it was all over. But if they called in the debt now, we would go bust, and there would be no future business. I told them that the international business was very strong and that they would soon get their money back, but not if they played hardball. I was delighted that both saw the wisdom in this win-win situation and, of course, they have been repaid many times over as we buy in excess of £15 million from them every year.

The final thing that happens in a CVA is the dreaded creditor's meeting. The administrator advertises the gathering and sends a notification to all outstanding creditors. If anyone turns up at the meeting who wants to shut down your company, then that's the end of it. We attended at the appointed time, and there was only one creditor who turned up, the Inland Revenue. He could see that the whole arrangement was genuine and went through the figures. He agreed not to pursue the debt, so the CVA went through, and the company was liquidated voluntarily.

It was fortunate that both Bar Code Systems (London), which I had recently formed to handle the acquisition of Axis, and International Bar Code Systems were still in business, so we carried on from there.

LIQUIDATION

It was a terribly stressful time because in addition to the liquidation, Liz was recovering from breast cancer treatment. A few months after incubation, the bank mysteriously summoned us to their headquarters in the city.

We sat in the waiting room for a good twenty minutes and asked ourselves what this could all be about. At last one of the secretaries appeared and said, "This way, please, Mr. and Mrs. Marcel. The board will see you now."

What! I gasped to myself. *If we're going in to see the board, this must be serious.*

They asked us to sit on one side of a huge, shiny table opposite six men in dark suits with stern looks. My stomach started to drop to the floor and my mouth went dry. I looked at Liz for her reaction. Her face was a delicate shade of white, which no doubt matched mine.

"You are overtrading," started the chairman, "which is illegal. You are breaking the law as directors and could go to prison." They thought we didn't have sufficient working capital to sustain the volume of business we were doing and wouldn't have enough working capital to pay our creditors, which is against the law.

You must be joking, I thought. *How could this be happening?* We had done nothing wrong.

"We will freeze your assets and send in an insolvency company to run your books."

We were so stunned we couldn't say anything. We left the boardroom shell-shocked. I thought about how rude and insensitive they were. They knew about Liz's condition.

Once the bank received the £400,000 from our debtors, they closed our accounts, withdrew their banking services, and cast us adrift.

We changed banks, but after we explained what had happened, they declined to give us overdraft privileges. That meant our business model had to change.

We put our international partners in direct contact with our suppliers, so they could buy direct, which meant that they saved the 15 percent margin that I'd been charging for my assistance to them. This left a big hole in our personal finances, so the partners replaced that with a consultant fee to make up for my loss.

> *They declined to give us overdraft privileges. That meant our business model had to change.*

My fabulous brother Michael lent me the money to purchase Axis's Film Master business and, sure enough, it made the extra profit forecast and a lot more over the years. We started a separate company together called Bar Code Systems (London) and put the Film Master and barcode label business in there. That way, Michael could be paid back as quickly as possible. He had a golden share, which gave him effective control over the new company to protect his investment. BCS London traded without an overdraft and continues to do so.

LESSONS LEARNED:

- Cash is king.

- Watch your cash flow every month and project it well in advance so there are no nasty surprises.

- Never forget that cash flow is the only game in town and that large revenues and profits often mean nothing.

- Learn about CVAs.

- Get sufficient financing.

- Beware of personal guarantees.

- Learn about overtrading even when things are going well.

QUESTIONS FOR YOU:

- Have you borrowed money for your business with a mortgage? Are you able to keep up the payments?

- Do you have an overdraft? Are you able to manage it?

- Do you have, and study, a statement of cash? Do you have a cash-flow projections spreadsheet?

9 HOW TO SURVIVE IN A MARKET WITHOUT SALES

After laying the groundwork during the first Scan Hungary, when we ran the event the following year, I met Tibor Szakacs, who ran a small software company. He seemed to fit in with my vision, so I formed BCS Hungary with him and two more shareholders who worked for him.

But things started to go wrong from the start. Tibor was more focused on his own business, so I had to replace him. While looking around for someone else to be my partner, I talked to a friend whose sales director was married to a Hungarian lady whose brother lived in Budapest.

I interviewed and hired the brother. His biggest strength seemed to be that he loved wine and was quite an expert on it—not exactly the best qualification for the job. Needless to say, he lasted only a few months, so I started to look around for yet another partner, but I didn't know anyone. Zoltan, one of the original shareholders, wanted the job, but I didn't think he was up to it. After all, he was a programmer. What did he know about managing a business?

Later, I received a lengthy letter from Zoltan applying for the job. My first instinct was to reject him, but before doing so, I showed the letter to Liz. She'd always been a great sounding board for me, especially when it came to dealing with people. She had a knack for understanding them and could put herself in their shoes, and she was known to resolve a number of staff problems before I could make the wrong decision.

To my surprise, when she read the letter, she encouraged me to give Zoltan the job. The letter, she asserted, was not from a person of weak character. There was a lot of passion in it, and the tone conveyed a sense of self-confidence. In addition, Zoltan presented a very good case for why I should take him on, and it wasn't because there was no one else! Liz said that for all we knew, he was the type of person who would be well respected in Hungary; and since he'd be taking instruction from me, there was only one way to find out if he would work out. So I gave Zoltan the job, and he proved himself capable a hundredfold.

FIND MORE PRODUCTS TO SELL

In 1992, there was virtually no interest in barcodes in Eastern Europe. All my friends and colleagues said I was an idiot for entering these markets. They said I was especially foolish to have given away control and that it would take years to get my money back. In fact, it took seven!

The banks refused to lend money for these ventures, so I had to finance it all myself. I was in it for the long term. My JV in Czechoslovakia, Kodys, ticked away quite nicely by selling labels, which paid the rent. But my partner in Russia, Sasha, wasn't interested in labels. Neither was Zoltan in Hungary. He didn't understand them.

One night after dinner together, I told Zoltan I was

> *The banks refused to lend money for these ventures, so I had to finance it all myself. I was in it for the long term.*

"promoting" him to be Mister Label, which meant he would now sell labels instead of software development. Today, that department represents 23 percent of his total business!

I modeled this activity on Bar Code Systems, where we had established a barcode label print bureau to take care of smaller print orders of up to seventy thousand labels, after which it was economical for the customer to buy his own printer. We would then sell the customer the printer and keep him supplied with blank labels and ribbons, which was a nice repeatable business, especially when sold with a one-year contract. This part of the business, along with Film Masters, paid for our overhead, so hardware sales contributed marginal profit.

An obvious attraction of Eastern Europe was the low cost of rent and salaries. I can't remember the exact figures, but the average salary was probably around $150 per month, so my overhead didn't break the bank. I sold a Film Master machine in Czechoslovakia (as it was still called then) and two in Moscow, but I couldn't find a customer in Hungary. These three sales, however, produced nice profits and gave me some working capital for Hungary.

But I had to develop a source of revenue from Hungary, and someone from my network in South Africa came to the rescue. Hal Adams was the buyer at IBM in Johannesburg, and I'd formerly sold OCR paper to him. He'd returned to the UK in the 1980s and took a senior position with Kores, a company that made carbon paper and cassette ribbons for computer printers. We'd kept in touch over the years and were good friends, plus Liz and his wife, Doreen, got on like a house on fire. We often spent Sundays at their home.

One day it struck me that we could sell his products in Hungary, so I asked if I could be his representative in that country. He agreed, and nobody was more surprised than I was when we got a huge order from the government

One day it struck me that we could sell his products in Hungary, so I asked if I could be his representative in that country.

for both carbon paper and ribbons. From there, we built up enough orders to warrant container loads of this stuff, and it soon became a nice little earner. Hal was very pleased that I'd found him a new, lucrative market.

Even better, our customers paid their bills. The culture in Eastern Europe was to pay cash on delivery. In their planned economy, the government dictated what to buy and how much to pay; and since the banks were government owned, there was no need for credit. Nor did anyone think they would ever need credit. That word was not in their vocabulary, just like *sell* wasn't.

In Russia, a timely opportunity came to us out of the blue in 1993. The Ukrainian supplier of bank-note-counting machines went bust and couldn't serve the banks. So Sasha called me and asked if I could locate some of these machines that we could sell. Well, why not?

Sasha called me and asked if I could locate some of these machines that we could sell. Well, why not?

I did some research and found two manufacturers in the US that agreed to provide us with the Tellermate machines; but they wanted us to pay via bill of lading, which meant that we had to deposit purchase money with a bank. The seller would collect when the bill of lading was accepted by the buyer as proof of delivery.

Sasha was a great salesman, and he seemed to know everyone. Thus, we started to sell many of these machines. He hired several disabled people to cold-call new Russian banks. The first order was for twenty Tellermate machines. The manufacturer wrote "Money Counters" as the product description on the documentation. When the boxes went through Russian customs, they were confiscated because the officials thought there was cash inside, and we didn't have permission to operate with cash!

That was the official version of the story, but Sasha later realized that the goods had been stolen, not confiscated, and they'd been sold to one of the new mafia banks to use in their currency-exchange offices. In fact, eventually someone in the Customs and Excise Ministry stole the whole business from us. Twenty handicapped people whom we employed lost their jobs, and we lost a great business.

Another product that interested Sasha was domestic cable. At that time, Russia wasn't a partner in the London Metal Exchange (LME), which meant that the country wasn't subject to the global price of metals. They could sell their metals and minerals at any price they liked, which was always about half the LME price. This was a great way for Russia to get hold of elusive foreign currency. Otherwise, they couldn't buy products from the West because nobody wanted to be paid in roubles!

Domestic cable was made of copper wire encased in a plastic sheath. The price of copper determined the cost of the cable, and from Russia, it was considerably cheaper than the current supplies. Through my network, I found a company that sold a large amount of domestic cable through do-it-yourself shops in the UK, and they were delighted to buy cable at a much cheaper rate.

This became a great business for us until one day when the factory in Moldova, where the cable was made, went on strike. Sixty of the employees, all women, lay down in front of the train with all my cable on it and stayed there for three days! This presented a serious risk factor to my customer, who started to doubt our ability to deliver. Shortly after that, there was an internal war, and the factory was burned down. Then Russia joined the LME, and our pot of gold went down the tubes.

STAND FIRM

Not long after, our business with Kores in Hungary also started to go wrong. Their factory was having serious production problems and started to ration the amount of product their customers could buy. I was rationed because they preferred to satisfy their UK customers rather than some weird country in Eastern Europe that they probably still thought of as Communist Russia, which caused my customers to become disgusted with my service.

Relations between Hal and me became quite strained because he didn't fulfill our orders, and, at one stage, four huge containers were delivered several weeks late. Hal expected me to pay for the lot, which was quite impossible. I didn't have the cash. Normally, they would have been delivered over a period of time and the proceeds of one container would pay for the next container and so on. Not only did I have to pay up because of these bills of lading that guaranteed payment, Hal either couldn't or wasn't prepared to extend the payment terms. I couldn't sell a lot of the products because my customers got fed up and found other suppliers, which left me with a great deal of stock that I either couldn't move or had to sell off at large discounts. This put a stop to the business and created a £100,000 loss in Hungary.

My brother encouraged me to close the business down and cut my losses, but I refused. I told Zoltan that in order to keep the business running, he'd have to pay all the money back before he received any dividends. Eventually, he did eventually repay me, but it took seven years. This proved what a good manager and partner he was. And now Hungary is one of the most profitable companies in the group, thanks to him.

LESSONS LEARNED:

- Surround yourself with a great team. This will help you command a good price when you sell the business. Entrepreneurs like to control everything and often don't learn the art of delegation. They must learn to empower their staff to manage their own issues and make their own decisions. They can be afraid to hire people who are smarter than they are because it makes them feel threatened in their own company. To run a successful business, you need an assortment of skills such as management, marketing, selling, technical, and financial. It's unusual to find all these in one person. Understand your own skills set, and hire for the others. It's impossible to innovate when there's no delegation.

- Don't be afraid to give equity to those partners who contribute to the business. It is better to have 50 percent of £5 million than 100 percent of £2 million. Consider Steve Jobs and Steve Wozniak of Apple. Wozniak was the inventor, and Jobs was the brains and the strategist. And then you can add a third, Jonathan Ives the designer. Other examples:

  - Bill Hewlett and Dave Packard of Hewlett Packard

  - Ben Cohen and Jerry Greenfield of Ben and Jerry's

  - Bill Gates and Paul Allen of Microsoft

  - Warren Buffett and Charlie Munger of Berkshire Hathaway

  - Larry Page and Sergey Brin of Google

  - Pierre Omidyar and Jeffrey Skoll of eBay

  - Michael Eisner and Frank Wells of Disney

- It's very lonely at the top, especially if you don't have anyone to discuss your ideas and strategy with. It makes you very insular. I was very fortunate to have my wife Liz in the business, but even then, I needed a great team. My big regret was that I didn't find someone to form as strong a partnership as those listed above, which may well have held back my company's potential.

- Eat humble pie and be open to the ideas of others. If I hadn't listened to Liz, I would never have found someone as good as Zoltan to run Hungary, which I can quantify in financial gain by adding up the last twenty years of profits!

- Be resourceful and go after new products in new markets. Don't be afraid of failure, even when you have setbacks. Get up and start over, and learn from what went wrong. No business is safe forever. You have to deliver on your promises, and you can't ever fully rely even on your best friends to bail you out, so be self-sufficient and cover your bases at all times.

- Don't be scared of big losses, provided you have people you can trust and are proven capable. You can stick with the vision and make it happen, no matter what. Can you imagine what it felt like to carry a £100,000 loss all those years ago in such an immature market!?

QUESTIONS FOR YOU:

- Do you micromanage and control everything in your company, or is the staff empowered to make decisions?

- Are you lucky to have a number two or equal partner? Who is your Steve Wozniak?

- Do you deliver on your promises?

10 GROW THE BUSINESS THROUGH NETWORKING

After a couple of years, we needed to expand our product line, as there was limited mileage in low-value, yet profitable, Film Masters. Supermarkets drove the growth in barcoding and insisted that they couldn't operate an economical scanning system unless a minimum of 80 percent of the products had barcodes printed on them. This was great for Film Master suppliers, as millions of different products needed barcodes!

But to ensure that the product scanned first time, the barcode had to be printed to exact specifications, and so the Film Master had to be produced to a very tight tolerance of +/- .005mm. To check the print accuracy, the *barcode verifier* was developed, which indicated whether the symbol would scan first time or not. If not, it showed if the problem was with the printing or packaging.

Just like the machines that plot the barcode on a Film Master are made by a handful of companies, so are verifiers. I was fortunate to get an exclusive agency for the UK from a

German company that produced a better device than the Quick Check, one of the first verifiers produced by my old company, Photographic Sciences, which we sold at the time.

TECHNOLOGICAL ADVANCES

Technology soon advanced, and the light pen powered by a light-emitting diode attached to the Quick Check and Ergi Check verifiers, was soon superseded by laser technology. Numeric Arts, our Film Masters supplier, sold such a device made by Symbol Technologies called Lasercheck. Symbol Technologies was the major manufacturer of barcode equipment and run by Jerome Swartz, a genius who invented the laser scanner as well as the laser verifier. He also invented the hand-held terminal, which scanned a barcode and stored the data for onward transmission to an external computer.

We agreed to start selling Lasercheck. It retailed at £10,000, was very heavy and bulky, and had to be lugged around in the car to the customer's site for a sales demonstration. It was very profitable to sell, and it helped us gain knowledge of the technology of barcoding and printing, which was essential to become a leader in the industry. This product gave us an edge and enabled us to become a trusted advisor of our customers. In fact, we reached our first £1 million after five years, which wasn't bad!

Soon after this, the thermal printer was invented. It had a two-inch-wide print head with microscopic electrodes that heated up and burned through a chemical coating on special paper to produce an image. This was perfect for barcodes, as the print head could produce the variable bar widths yet still produce a blue or black image on white paper, so the scanner could read the contrast.

It was obvious that this could pose a threat or an opportunity to our Film Master business: multiple barcode labels could be printed at high speed and stuck on products, which eliminated the need for Film Masters. Also, if you packed different products in the same type of packaging, you'd have to print different bar-codes for each type, which meant smaller and more costly print runs. It was more economical just to use the thermal printer to produce a barcoded sticky label and affix it to the common pack for each change of product.

We contracted with a supplier to sell their thermal printers, which was the catalyst to starting our own barcode-label print bureau where we could offer customers a choice; they could either buy a printer from us, or they could buy their labels from our bureau. The break-even was about 75,000 labels.

———

I have always believed that *people buy people*. That makes perfect sense because would you rather buy from someone you liked or someone you didn't know? To become *liked*, you need to become *known*, and this is where network-ing comes in.

> **To become liked, you need to become known, and this is where networking comes in.**

The important thing about networking that most people fail to understand is that you're there to *build relationships*. People buy from people they like, but before they can like you, they have to get to know you. The prob-lem with most networkers is that they talk about themselves too much. They seldom pause for breath to ask you a question. That won't make anyone like you.

The secret to being a good networker starts with exchang-ing business cards. After that, you'll be asked what you do. The proper response is to deliver your "elevator speech." Imagine you get in an elevator with the CEO of a company you've been tar-geting for months, and it is just the two of you for the next forty seconds or so. What would you say?

After your "elevator pitch," you immediately ask him/her what she does. Hopefully, you'll get a similar, concise answer from that person rather than their life story. Your job is to probe, listen, and question to see if there is any mutual business interest. If not, move on to the next person. It's not rude to do so. In fact, it's expected.

Once you find a prospect, don't try to sell them anything. Just explore their likes/dislikes, history, birthday, and so on. Ask if they're a member of LinkedIn or any other networking sites, then connect with them. Send them articles or blogs you've written or links to things that might interest them, which could even be their hobbies. Thus, you are building an empathetic relationship, which might lead to business in a few months.

KEEP CURRENT

Since the barcode industry and its technology was changing rapidly, it was important for me to keep abreast of what the competition was up to and to network within the industry. If I didn't know what was going on, how could I react or be pro-active?

> *Since the barcode industry and its technology was changing rapidly, it was important for me to keep abreast of what the competition was up to and to network within the industry.*

This is when I joined our industry association, Automatic Identification of Manufacturers UK (AIM UK), a vibrant organization with about fifty members. We had a charismatic leader, Ian Smith, who ran it. He was also controversial. Smith played a large part in growing the industry in the UK and Europe.

At our first annual members meeting, the chairman asked me to be the vice-chairman for that year, which surprised me because we had met only a few months before. But I accepted, knowing that it meant I'd be the chairman the next year. It fit well with my intention of doing my part to help grow the industry. The culture of the industry was to compete in a friendly manner and grow the pie, so we could each have a bigger slice, rather than try to kill each other off.

Becoming vice-chairman was a great decision, and I became very active. One of the first things I did in the role was to organize our first trade industry show, called Scantech UK, named after the one in the States. I'd had wonderful experiences at the event in the States. Each year, Scantech took place in a different city.

One story stands out; it was in San Jose, California, in 1987. That day, I drove out to see a potential customer and then came back to visit the show in the afternoon. I was on the show floor speaking to a colleague, when we both looked up at the ceiling. We'd heard the loud screech of a jet plane as it came in to land. This was not unusual because the airport wasn't far away, and we'd heard similar noises throughout the day.

But as I looked up, I saw the large, round sound dampeners that hung from the ceiling sway from side to side. First, they swayed to the far end of the hall, and then they started to sway toward me. At the same time, I felt the ground shift. We all stopped talking and looked at each other.

It struck me that we were having an earthquake. I felt very scared. I pictured great crevasses opening up and falling into one. For some reason—maybe sixth sense—I remembered reading a book about earthquakes that said to stand in a solid structure, such as a doorway, until it passed. It seemed that others had read the same book because many people headed for the various exits. By the time we got there, the noise had stopped, as well as the shaking. No crevasses or debris were evident.

We went down the stairs with great care and looked up and sideways in case there was loose debris or even metal struts that had become dislodged. I was concerned that some such thing might fall on us, but we got to ground level safely. As we exited the building, an extraordinary sight awaited. The huge fountain in the front, which had been pushing out plumes of water when

I went in, was now completely empty. The water was nowhere to be seen.

We walked back to our hotel and marveled at the lack of damage. Things looked relatively normal except for a few dislodged bricks here and there. It was a real tribute to Californian engineers and architects. Our hotel was dark. We couldn't go up in the elevator, of course, so I took the stairs to my room. As I opened the door, I imagined the chaos I'd find—perhaps broken windows, clothes all over the floor, and cracked mirrors. But the only damage was to the TV, which had fallen to the floor from its table.

Everyone was pretty shaken up by all this, so we were delighted to accept an invitation to a cocktail party given by one of our suppliers. That calmed my nerves, but only for a short while. Later when I watched CNN, they reported that the highway I'd driven that morning was now a twisted wreck. Fifty people had died, the sole casualties of the earthquake. There but for the grace of God went I.

I was soon made chairman of AIM UK, president of AIM Europe, and president of AIM International, which meant a fair amount of travel and meetings. Our goals were to increase membership and to make the annual Scantech UK show successful. These exhibitions were a great place to network and meet fellow members of the industry. It was also a great place to meet the competition and see what all the latest hardware was about.

LESSONS LEARNED:

- Travel as much as you can. Travel allows you to network, build great relationships, meet new people, and experience different cultures.

- When networking, learn how to ask questions and build relations. Listen more than you talk.

- Look out for any threats to your business. Try to live with them and adapt.

- *People buy people*, and your reputation is everything. In the old days, it wasn't *what* you knew, but *whom* you knew. In today's social-media world, prospective customers ask around to find out who knows you and has done business with you. They also check your Twitter and Facebook pages, so make sure there's nothing embarrassing in your social-media accounts.

- Be outgoing and positive.

QUESTIONS FOR YOU:

- Remember a time when you went to a networking function. Did you tell your life story to everyone, or did you start to build relationships?

- Have you ever gotten a new customer through networking?

- Take a look at your Facebook page. Is there anything embarrassing there? If so, take it down; you never know who may see it. It's a very small world.

11 *KEEP REACHING!*

O nce I started expanding into Eastern Europe, I couldn't be stopped. I had joint ventures in Hungary, Czechoslovakia, and Russia. My next interests were in Poland, Bulgaria, former Yugoslavia, Romania, and Ukraine.

In 1993, the two republics that made up Czechoslovakia decided to split. They became the Czech Republic and the Slovakian Republic, or Slovakia. Many companies now had offices on both sides of former Czechoslovakia that were governed by different laws. In effect, they now had separate identities.

> **Once I started expanding into Eastern Europe, I couldn't be stopped.**

After a couple of years, Zdenek, my Czech partner, thought we needed to have an office in Slovakia to deal with companies there who no longer wanted to trade with the Czech Republic. He had a friend, Stanislav Čierny, who owned an office products company in Bratislava, the capital of Slovakia, who was interested in a joint venture.

One morning I arrived at Kodys, our Czechoslovakian JV, at 9:00 a.m. I was introduced to a tall, slim gentleman who was slightly younger than me. He had a thin face and a moustache; he looked a bit like an Austrian cavalryman. We sat down at the table to discuss business, and he pulled out a strange looking bottle of what I assumed was alcohol. He offered me a drink! I couldn't believe he wanted to drink so early in the morning, but he told me it was to celebrate our new joint venture. After we drained the bottle of Demänovka—a delicious drink made of fourteen different herbs—the deal was done and Kodys Slovensko was born.

POLAND

Sasha and Zdenek introduced me to their counterpart in Warsaw, Poland, and I persuaded him quite easily to purchase my Film Master generator. But I didn't think him suitable as a joint-venture partner because he was not his own boss and was focused on printing. He introduced me to Grzegosz Szyska, the head of the Institute of Warehousing in Poznan, who would be right for the systems side, while Pawel Korczak, whom I knew from a label printing company in Wroclaw, would be good for the label side. I had hoped that Grzegosz would introduce us to a lot of customers through his position, especially as he was involved in the Polish GS1—the agency that issued the barcode numbers—but nothing materialized. So I gave it up after a couple of years without ever formalizing any JV.

Poland, in fact, was a bit of a failure for me. I went from prospective partner to prospective partner and didn't find anyone suitable.

————

As you establish yourself in business through the years, your network should continue to grow and include those from years past, as well as new connections. It was the former that helped me expand into Poland.

I met Andrew Miedzanowsky Sinclair when I lived in South Africa, where he manufactured cookware similar to Le Creuset, the famous French brand. Andrew was tall, large, and loud and had enormous charisma. You couldn't fail to notice him in a room.

Eventually, he left South Africa to live in England. Since he was both a consultant *and* Polish, I asked him to accompany me on some trips to Poland to see if we could find prospective partners.

As you establish yourself in business through the years, your network should continue to grow and include those from years past, as well as new connections.

Andrew was well-connected, with an amazing background. He was the youngest ever leader of the Polish Resistance in World War II when he sent the Germans packing out of Poland. One particular story was when he was positioned on the roof of a hospital with his rifle, sniping at the Germans. A bullet found its mark and took off his left finger and part of his hand. He escaped from the roof and went to the hospital, where they fixed his hand and sheltered him for six weeks until the Germans gave up their search for him.

———

In 1998, my business development manager, whose job it was to find me partners and support the current ones, told me about a couple of young guys he'd met when he visited a company called Optimus IC. At the time, this was the biggest PC and POS company in Poland. It was run by Jarek Ćwikła as managing director and Łukasz Iwanczewski as his sales director. As we sat in Łukasz's office, he explained his role at Optimus. He was very good looking—had blond hair and a good attitude—and it was clear he was a successful salesman. I persuaded him to let us meet with his boss, Jarek, who was the details man. I invited them to pack up their nice, steady jobs to start BCS Poland—a step into the unknown!

They played hard to get, so I thought that if I could get them to meet some of the JV partners, they might be persuaded to join us. I invited them to our annual IBCS conference in Ireland, where we always have a team-building afternoon.

Jarek and Łukasz were swayed by the fun and camaraderie, so they agreed to leave their jobs and join us. There was only one minor problem. They both lived in Nowy Sącz, a town in the southern Poland, about five hours drive from Warsaw, where most of the action was. So in addition to an HQ in Nowy Sącz, we needed to have an office in Warsaw, which duplicated some of our costs. BCS Poland has grown and grown due to them, so I'm thankful for their decision.

BULGARIA

Next up was Bulgaria. As president of AIM Europe, I was invited to speak at a seminar for the chamber of commerce in Sofia. In fact, my position in AIM Europe got me quite a few invitations with great networking outcomes, like in Tel Aviv, Israel, where I addressed two hundred businessmen.

It was at the conference in Sofia that I met with three share-holders from a company called Uvicom: Villian Koulev, Yuri Dimitrov and Anatolyi Atanasov. All three were interested in barcodes, and we kept in touch. A few years later, they received a request from Metro Cash and Carry for a barcode system. At the time, Metro was the only Western chain in Bulgaria. I flew over to meet with the customer, and the four of us did a great presentation that led to an order large enough to finance BCS Bulgaria in partnership with Uvicom.

There are some great software programmers in Bulgaria, and BCS Bulgaria has written some terrific applications for direct store delivery and utility meters. Unfortunately, Uvicom is based in Varna, a city on the Black Sea coast. Since most business was conducted in Sofia, the capital, we needed to open an office there as well.

ROMANIA

As far as Romania was concerned, I was very keen to get a JV there because Liz and I had adopted our daughter, Jess, from Romania. One of the people connected with that was John Condurateanu, who contacted AIM to represent them in Romania. His son, Bogdan, was very bright, tall, and lanky, and he was ranked seventh in his computer class at university.

One year, Bogdan came to live with us in London to help look after baby Jess. I taught him the barcode ropes so he could start BCS Romania when he got back. That's what he tried to do, but another company beat him to it. In fact, they even called themselves Bar Code Systems! I met their managing director at an exhibition one time, and he explained that he'd always admired me, so he named his company after mine. I'm not sure that was the reason; he probably wanted to keep me out of Romania.

We did talk JV, but by this time he already had twenty-four people working for him, mostly software developers. It was out of my range and didn't conform to my startup criteria, so it never worked out. Some years later, he invited me to buy into his company, and I went to Bucharest to chat about it. When he told me that two government employees had invested, I backed off. I could smell corruption. I was proven right and, in fact, the company defaulted on a large debt to their supplier, Symbol.

BCS Hungary does occasional deals with some Hungarians in the eastern part of Romania, but that's the closest I get now—a big regret.

———

There were a couple of scary incidents on my visits to Eastern Europe, but if you consider the fresh state of their economies and their emergence from communism, it's a surprise that there weren't more.

I always like to get to the airport at the last minute, much to the consternation of my travel companions. After all, there's work to be done, and time spent at airports is unproductive.

On one such occasion, Zdenek, my Czech partner, drove me to the airport in Prague with just ten minutes to spare. He drove right up to the terminal entrance instead of the car park. I thanked him, grabbed my overnight bag, and dashed out of the car—only to run into a masked man holding a machine gun! I guess my adrenaline was in full flow, so I didn't stop and put my hands up as expected. I dashed around the gunman and ran toward the terminal entrance, a little over thirty feet away. To the right was someone lying prone on the ground. Another masked man pointed a machine gun down toward him, while a couple of other masked men stood around and watched.

I ran into the terminal and made the flight with seconds to spare, but I have no idea what happened to the potential kidnappers outside. Zdenek didn't find out either. He drove away as quickly as possible.

On another occasion—also in Prague—I hopped in a taxi around midnight with Ian Smith from AIM Europe to go back to our hotel. All was fine until we got there. Instead of parking in front of the entrance, the driver stopped short. He turned around and said, "Pay what's on the meter."

Ian and I had been deep in conversation, so I hadn't looked at the meter until then. This trip should have cost about sixty crowns, but the meter read 620 crowns!

"Ian," I whispered, "do you see what this chap is charging us? Either it is a mistake or a rip off."

"No," I said to the driver, "that is a mistake. It should be sixty crowns."

"If you don't pay," he growled, "I will take you to my leader."

I turned to Ian and whispered, "I have no intention to pay this, so let's just jump out of the cab."

At this point, the driver started to reverse at full speed, then did a quick about-turn to go back the other way. He accelerated down to the main road, which had no traffic.

We were both startled and scared, and I wondered what on earth we could do about it. The cab sped off into the night, destination unknown, with a goodness-knows-what threat hanging over us. *How are we to get out of this?* I wondered.

About ten minutes later, I saw a sharp bend up ahead and a plan started to formulate.

"Ian," I whispered, "there's a bend in the road coming up, and he will have to slow down. Be prepared to jump out when I open the door."

Just then, the car slowed. I opened the door and threw myself out of the car, which by now had slowed down, so I didn't hurt myself. When I stopped rolling, I came to a standstill right at a policeman's feet.

Well, that's a bit of luck, I thought. I started to explain in English that the taxi driver had tried to kidnap us and so on, but he didn't understand English.

By that time Ian had exited the car safely and he came over. I was surprised and shocked to see that the cab had stopped at the corner and the driver was getting out. I would have expected him to see the policeman and hightail it out of there. Instead, he wandered over to us and stood on my foot!

What the hell? I thought. Meanwhile, the policeman and the driver spoke at length in Czech. I was told to pay the driver sixty crowns, which I did—reluctantly. The driver sped off, and I saw the policeman's car parked nearby, so I asked if he would give us a lift to our hotel.

"No," he said. "You'll have to get a taxi."

I would have laughed if it weren't so unfunny. It was late and the streets were deserted. We did manage to find another taxi soon after and got to the hotel in one piece.

I told Zdenek about our adventure the next day, and he said we were very lucky. We'd been picked up by a Mafia cab, he explained, and the driver was probably taking us to the Mafia boss, where we would have been beaten up, robbed, and dumped somewhere. Zdenek told me that the policeman was a silent accomplice because he allowed the taxi driver to go on his way.

Another incident that had a different kind of scare occurred in an early trip to Moscow. Russia has the costliest of hotels, even though they are not up to Western standards. So Sasha used to get me into the President Hotel, which had only opulent suites, in keeping with the exclusive use by the Politburo. My room had a huge four-poster bed, sofas, and gold faucets on the bath and basins. The food was also quite good, and we always started our meals with champagnski and the obligatory vodka— or two or three.

One night, I returned to my room at about one o'clock in the morning. As I exited the elevator, the door to the guest room on the other side of the hall opened, and two very glamorous young Russian ladies emerged. They made a beeline for me and asked if I would like to entertain them in my room. It was clear that they were fresh from another client and were still in the mood for a bit of fun! Difficult to refuse!

YUGOSLAVIA

In 1991, my cousin, John Rubin, and I drove overnight to Belgrade from Budapest to explore some partnerships there, but I couldn't find anyone suitable. Later on, I traveled to Slovenia to visit Spica, with branches in most of the countries around there, and developed a long relationship with Tone Stanovnik, a medical doctor who wanted us to market one of his software solutions. It never took off, but we agreed not to encroach on his territory. In return, he wouldn't come into ours. Together, we more or less covered all the countries east of Austria. We talked of a merger/acquisition many times, but we couldn't find a way forward together.

UKRAINE

I found a partner in Lviv in Ukraine, not far from my main office in Poland. It was a small company, and I sold them some Film Masters for a time. Ukraine is a huge country, so it would have been great to have a partner, particularly in Kiev, but once again, I couldn't find anyone suitable.

Lviv is memorable for one unfortunate incident, which was also scary! We took off for Krakow, Poland, in a two-engine prop plane from LOT Polish airlines. Something seemed to go wrong immediately after takeoff. We didn't climb very high and then started to circle around. I sat next to the window and kept seeing the same buildings pass beneath every five minutes or so! I asked the air hostess what had happened, and she said that the flaps got stuck, so we needed to land back at Lviv. We got lower and lower to the ground, and I found myself amazingly calm as we started our final approach—that is, until I saw four fire engines lined up near the runway! I understandably got a bit nervous, but we managed to land safely.

LESSONS LEARNED:

- Prepare for the unexpected when you go into the unknown, but enjoy the experience.

- Communicate and be friends with your competitors. These days, you can't do everything yourself, and you need to build up an ecosystem of people and companies with complementary skills.

- Our industry is comprised of small companies, and we don't have the resources to build huge teams. So collaboration is the name of the game. We often introduce a smaller company to a customer, and they act as a part of our group. As long as the customer is serviced according to our standards, then it's possible to split the profits to everyone's satisfaction. If you provide a complementary service to another vendor, then you may have access to their leads as well as your own. They may well want to use you in their solutions, which is a win-win. In the old days, we were all too protective of our skills and customers, but now that has changed for the better.

QUESTIONS FOR YOU:

- Do you have an ecosystem? If not, should you have one, and who should be part of it?

- Are you in the state of mind to collaborate with your competition? Do you see any value in this?

12   USE PROVEN MARKETING TOOLS TO GROW

Every growth business needs to understand marketing, so in 1973, I went to the Graduate School of Business in Cape Town, South Africa, to get my first taste of it. There I became acquainted with the four Ps of marketing—product, place, price, and promotion—which I still use to this day. The four Ps insist that you have the right product in the right place for the right price and delivered on time. But first you must determine your target market, what you think they need, and how you'll promote your product or service to them.

I've often debated with people inside and outside my company whether to combine the sales and marketing functions in one person or department. My view is *definitely not!* Sales and marketing involve different functions, and different skills are needed. Marketing requires a person to generate leads from the target markets, which means they need to research the market and maintain an objective view on the customers. This is an internal position. They don't sell anything; they qualify leads before they pass them to the salesperson. The salesperson must follow up on the leads and close the deal, so this is an external position. They should pound the pavement and visit potential customers. Combining the two functions may save money, but how can one person be marketing when he or she should be out of the office selling?

Sales and marketing involve different functions, and different skills are needed.

It wasn't difficult to define my target market: anybody who needed a barcode on their product. That included manufacturers of retail products, package designers, packaging printers and suppliers, label manufacturers and suppliers, and the supermarkets themselves. Very conveniently, these were the same targets that would buy our verifiers, labels, and printers.

BRANDING

It was very important to establish a brand, and Liz and I chose the tiger to represent Bar Code Systems. Why? Liz used to call me Tigger after the character in *Winnie the Pooh* because I was always bouncy; and since a tiger has black stripes, there was a loose connection to barcoding.

Our tiger went through various phases as we evolved as a company. It started as rather a whimsical tiger drawn freehand, then we put him in the jungle facing out, looking through vertical reeds that looked like barcodes. As we became a more serious company, we looked for a more serious tiger. We found a great photo of a tiger on all fours with his head up looking to the right. He was very proud, with black stripes on a yellowy-brown body. It was important to find a real tiger, but nothing too fierce that would scare the customers. We wanted a tiger that looked confidant and friendly.

The tiger was there to enshrine our values as a company. In fact, we use it in Bulgaria, Hungary, and Poland, but not for the two Kodys in Czechoslovakia because Zdenek didn't like it. We printed the logo on little labels that had our phone number and address, and we stuck them on the bottom of all our hardware and at the end of our reels of labels.

It was very sad when Zdenek Vonasek passed away from cancer in 2010. His sales director Jan Prihoda (Honza) had been working with us for a long time as sales director and was able to take over as my Czech partner.

MESSAGING

Early on, I spent a great deal of time wandering around super-market shelves to look for products without barcodes. When I found them, I called the manufacturer to arrange a meeting, so I could explain that they needed to barcode their products in order to keep them on the supermarket shelves. Of course, I suggested they buy from us!

Our message was that we took the mystique out of barcodes. We talked to our prospects about how to apply barcodes in a way that wasn't threatening. We knew they were nervous about the implementation because it was new territory for them. Some feared that they would lose their job if things went wrong, so we were always there as a friendly and knowledgeable partner whose hand they could hold.

It was a very valuable message, especially when we started to sell verifiers. Verifiers were used to test the barcodes to make sure they scanned the first time, which was important to avoid long lines at the checkout because the technology didn't work. Using the verifier, the store would scan the printed barcode symbol and get a report about any deviation from tolerance that the bar/spaces and colors might show. After that, it was up to the printer to correct any deviations.

I made it my business to learn every single nuance about the barcode, which included all the encodations of the different sym-bologies and their construction, as well as all the different print processes and how each substrate was affected by ink pressure and different color combinations. I trained my salespeople and some of the technicians. There was no problem they couldn't solve.

Because the verifier machine was too expensive to buy sight unseen, when we demonstrated it to potential customers, our message was powerful. We cared about our customers and it showed. Soon, we became the dominant player.

> **We cared about our customers and it showed. Soon, we became the dominant player.**

In the early 1990s, we shifted direction and just sold printers and scanners with a bit of label design software. This enabled a customer to open a template on his or her computer screen and add a barcode in various shapes, sizes, graphics. The text could be moved around in boxes, and the barcode could then be sent to the printer to produce labels. The pain was to get it to print. The connection was an RS232—the plug on each piece of hardware that had to be connected by a cable. The connections weren't stable and often varied from device to device, so we capitalized on that opportunity and started to install the equipment for our customers.

WEBSITES

It wasn't till the mid-1990s that we could build websites to show and sell our wares. Before then, we needed other showcases to strut our stuff. The tools we used for the *promotion* part of the marketing mix were exhibitions, public relations, newsletters, brochures, seminars, and direct mail. We didn't have social media or email—or even digital marketing—in those days.

> **Our solution was to target the customer better than anyone else and to personalize our messages.**

"How on earth did you sell anything?" I hear you cry. Our solution was to target the customer better than anyone else and to personalize our messages. We touched the customer at many points and didn't have to worry that our emails didn't reach the right person or ended up in the spam tray or recycle bin.

SEMINARS

In Eastern Europe, seminars were very successful. In the Czech Republic, Kodys organized their first seminar at a five-star hotel in the center of Prague. I opened it up with a keynote speech. At that time, my partner didn't understand why we spent such a large amount of money to present to only fifty people; but feedback from the delegates indicated that they appreciated that an "English gentleman" had come to Prague just to make a presentation to them. My partner now understood that the event helped Kodys increase its reputation, and we've held many more such customer events since then.

But our most effective tool was exhibitions, where we distributed small booklets that explained the barcode system in simple terms. We also used product brochures and a corporate brochure. Needless to say, all the competitors tried to outdo each other with these, but our little factual booklets were different because they provided very good information that took the mystery out of barcoding. Every year, we participated in five main exhibitions.

EXHIBITIONS

Ultimately, we changed our offer to be more competitive and started to offer a total solution rather than just parts of the solution. We marketed ourselves as a one-stop shop, and to introduce this, we launched our new service at a logistics exhibition on a cruise ship that sailed up and down the French coast and the Channel Islands for three days.

Exhibitors paid for a small space, which consisted of a table and two chairs in one of the lounges, and the fee we paid determined which lounge, dining room, and quality of cabin we got. I always took my systems manager, Neil Keighley, with me and paid for the most expensive level, the equivalent of first class on a cruise.

The delegates paid nothing. Most came from blue-chip companies, and exhibitors could nominate whom we wanted to invite. All the senior people in their companies, such as logistics and operations directors, as well as a few managing directors, were invited. Business was conducted at prearranged one-on-one meetings during business hours that lasted thirty minutes.

Exhibitors got a list of delegates in advance, and the delegates got a list of exhibitors, and you ticked a box next to the names of the people you wanted to meet. You could also cross out anyone you didn't want to meet, in case they requested time with you. The organizers matched things up and produced a list of meeting times.

It was such a thrill to see the agenda and who had agreed to meet with you. Between Neil and me, our agenda consisted of ninety-nine slots, which included meal times. We bought the delegates' meals—three delegates per meal—and in the evening, we wore black tie and took them to the onboard casino after dinner. We usually met over ninety customers during the event.

The first thing we did was to go straight to the purser to get our list of meetings, which we took back to our cabin to see who had accepted our invitation—and, more importantly, who refused!

"Hey, Neil. Look, we've got the logistics director from Unichem—one of our targets. And the IT director of DHL. But we have two gaps at dinner tomorrow and two more before coffee the next day. Let's figure out whom we still want to meet with who isn't on the list."

Then we filled in a blue slip with the name of the delegate and the time and room where we wanted to meet. We took the blue slips, or "love notes," as I called them, to the purser to deliver. I called them love notes because we intended to invite them to a date with lots of love to get their business. Then came the fun as we waited for the replies. Would they accept or make an excuse not to see us?

It was such a brilliant concept that we did it for many years in a row. In fact, we were the organizer's best client. It was quite expensive—and a big risk—but it always paid for itself. Our best customers came from the event, including Western Power and Unichem.

Western Power asked us to write an inventory management solution for a small unmanned warehouse that housed strange tools. Their engineers would be given a job that needed these tools, so they went to the warehouse to get them, took them out to the job, then put them back at the end of the day. The order system we wrote tracked the products picked and put in a box to fulfill an order. These solutions led to many other variables and customers that wanted similar solutions.

MARKETING PLAN

One of the great marketing tools I use is called HEMP, as discussed in *The Highly Effective Marketing Plan*, a book by Peter Knight. The main thrust is to focus on the *story* of your product or service and to identify the one big thing that makes it unique. Then base your marketing on that. Too many people think of all the *features* of their product or service rather than the *benefits* when it's the benefits a customer will buy. If you focus on that one big benefit, you'll have a winner.

DIGITAL STRATEGIES

Most companies now have a digital-marketing strategy where most marketing is done online, but not just using websites. They leverage digital channels such as Google search; social media such as Facebook, LinkedIn, and Twitter; as well as email to connect with their current and prospective customers. Most have a CRM (customer relationship management) system to do this such as Salesforce.com. Campaigns can be better targeted and tracked using these systems; so although the cost per lead has increased, the conversion-to-customer rate has also increased.

LESSONS LEARNED:

- Turn yourself into a brand from which you can define your culture and values. Everyone in your organization should adhere to those values and behave accordingly.

- Embrace the four Ps of marketing: product, place, promotion, and price.

- Learn about HEMP, the highly effective marketing plan, by visiting http://phoenixplc.com/hemp.html.

- Be flexible with your business model and adapt to market circumstances. Don't be rigid; always be prepared to change. Charles Darwin said, "It is not the strongest of the species that survives, nor the most intelligent; it is the one that is most adaptable to change."

- Employ a dedicated social-media person who understands Google AdWords, Facebook ads, Twitter, and LinkedIn.

- Have an overall digital marketing strategy as well as using the four Ps; they are complementary.

QUESTIONS FOR YOU:

- Does your company have a brand identity?

- Do you have a marketing plan?

- What's the first thing to think about when marketing a product?

13 IMPROVE YOUR BUSINESS KNOWLEDGE

I f you want to grow your business, you must keep abreast of the best business practices and especially stay on top of new technologies. One reason we were successful is that every company, big or small, could use our solutions.

Think about how barcodes have changed the world. At its rawest edge, it's about inventory control. Warehouse managers will tell you that they have 99 percent accurate inventory; but when you drill down, it's probably about 92 percent accurate. For those who can admit that they don't know where everything is, it can be as low as 60 percent!

So what are the effects of inaccurate inventory? Customer service is impacted, for one, because if you haven't got the right stock to fulfill orders—or maybe not enough of it—customers will get frustrated and go somewhere else. Perhaps your warehouse is full of dead stock that is obsolete. In fact, lots of negative things associated with dead stock leads to incorrect stock valuations on the balance sheet and loss of bottom-line profits as this stock was forecast to sell not knowing it was obsolete and couldn't sell.

The accurate warehouse drives supply-chain solutions all over the world and helps companies operate at maximum efficiency and profit. Warehouse control is a compelling reason to use barcodes. As Sir Terry Leahy, a recent chairman of the supermarket Tesco said, "Without barcodes we don't have a business." Our salespeople, therefore, always got a welcome from prospective customers because we always had a solution to offer.

PURSUE BEST PRACTICES

From the very beginning, I had to teach the Eastern European joint ventures how to run their companies and to learn the best business practices from the West. One way was to join a global CEO support group called Vistage.

Vistage members learn everything about each other's businesses so they work together to solve everyday issues using the group experience. We met once a month. More often than not, I learned some very useful business tools. I share some of them with you below.

Make or Break opened up the world of dashboards to me, a form of business intelligence. My computer screen displayed—in visual form—how the company was performing against its key performance indicators. Red alerted me to a problem, amber was a warning, and green meant that all was fine. The metrics were updated in real time, so the performance of my company was always at my fingertips. New versions of Excel can now do this extremely effectively.

Make or Break asked me to think about the one thing that had to be done extraordinarily well to achieve my vision. Once I'd defined that, I created the value chain of activities to make it happen and then used a spreadsheet and dashboards to measure the progress.

I learned a long time ago that *what gets measured gets done.*

It's important to have a measurable target that motivates you to achieve it. In fact, I recommend you write down all the key performance indicators in your company for every department, including finance, operations, sales, manufacturing. and marketing. Create a dashboard for each one, and ask your managers to report the results to you every month.

Here are the dashboards that we use:

- **Solution Stacks:** This dashboard measures what percentage of software and services we sell compared to hardware. Our target is 40 percent hardware and 30 percent for both services and software.

- **Marketing Dashboard:** This dashboard tracks the number of customers we call on in the top, middle, and bottom tier of our marketing pyramid per month compared to our target.

- **Competitors' Customers:** We measure how many we call on each month compared to the target.

- **Solution Training:** This shows what percentage of our salespeople are trained in solutions and have taken regular exams that measure their knowledge.

- **Critical Success Factors That Lead to a Sale:** This dashboard shows what we are doing to generate sales. We measure the number of leads that generate a number of qualifying phone calls, which lead to a number of appointments, then to a number of visits, leading to a number of proposals, leading to numbers of sales, and then the average sale per proposal. Measuring these factors produces much better performance from the sales team because they know we're keeping track of such key performance indicators.

The concept of *consultative selling* was one of the most powerful sales techniques I learned from a Vistage speaker from a consultancy called SBR. When a salesperson started selling *solutions* rather than *hardware*, he or she needed a completely different sales approach. The methodology is called QUIS: Question, Understanding, Influence, and Solidify. When we changed our business model to become an application solution integrator, we needed to change our whole culture from being hardware-oriented to solution-oriented. I soon banned the words *product* and *hardware* unless they were spoken in the same breath as *software* and *services*.

QUIS is very straightforward. Here are the steps:

1. Question the customer about their needs and what keeps them awake at night. Then dig down to…

2. Understand their real pain and relate it back to them so they know you understand their issues. To be even more professional, you can translate back to them what *they actually do need* rather than what *they think they need*. Then you can bring out your presentation to…

3. Influence them to buy from you. Finally…

4. Solidify and agree on the next steps.

Another brilliant tool is Break-Even Percentage in Terms of Sales. This tells you how financially safe your company is; and at the same time, it gives you an easy formula to make it even safer. Investment decisions can be tested within this framework.

So how does it work? Using this method, you can change just three figures in your profit and loss when you implement certain strategies. These figures represent sales, gross margin, and overhead.

For example, take a forecast profit-and-loss spreadsheet for the year and write down those three figures:

Sales are £**100**, margin is **50** percent, and overhead is £**50**.

The break-even % = overhead /margin %

so **50/50** x **100** = 100%.

This is also your break-even point, but no one wants to break even. That's not enough to keep your company safe. In fact, the safe break-even target is 80 percent of sales, which gives you some wiggle room for unexpected situations and underperformance.

So how do we achieve 80 percent of sales? As mentioned before, you can just change the sales, gross margin, and overhead figures—or any combination of the three. First, let's change the sales figure to achieve this magic ratio.

Sales are £**120**, margin is **50** percent, and overhead is £**50**.
50/50 x 100 = 100/120 = 83.3% of sales.

Next, try changing the margin figure:

Sales are £**100**, margin is **52** percent, and overhead is £**50**.
50/52 x 100 = 96/120 is 80% of sales.

If increasing margin is too difficult to achieve, you can try to reduce overhead:

Sales are £**100**, margin is **52** percent, and overhead is £**40**.
40/50 x 100 = 80% of sales.

This may take some time to absorb, but it's a powerful tool and worth it in the end.

It's also useful to determine if you can afford to hire new staff. For example, if break-even percent is 70 percent of sales, you can add a salesperson's salary to the overhead and then recalculate the break-even percentage. If it comes to around 80 percent, you can hire another salesperson Naturally, you can calculate any of these combinations to ascertain which are the easiest options that will give you +/-80%.

PERSONAL DEVELOPMENT SEMINARS

In 2012, I received a free ticket to the Excel Centre in London to hear some inspirational speakers, including Lord Sebastian Coe, one of our famous Olympic sprinters who is now a hero for being in charge of the successful London 2012 Olympic games. Several of the other speakers were well known, although not to me, including Tony Robbins. I'd never heard of him.

When I arrived, the place was totally packed. There must have been over a thousand people there, which seemed strange because these events normally only attract about a hundred people. There was a huge amount of excitement and anticipation in the room, which I could feel from the moment I entered.

I took my seat, and at the appointed time some terrific rock music started to blare out. Everyone got up out of their seats and started to dance and sway to the music, being warmed up by some chap who came on the stage to get them going. *For what?* I wondered. This was hardly what I expected from this unknown motivational speaker.

And then an enormous giant of a man entered stage right. He was dressed all in black with an open-neck shirt and a head microphone. He clapped his hands vigorously and leaped about on stage, whirling his disciples into a frenzy—and it was only nine o'clock in the morning! This was Tony Robbins. Oh my God, could I feel the energy pumping inside him as he pushed it across the airwaves towards his adoring audience. This was like nothing I had ever experienced before. Wow! He had me at "hello"!

He started off by telling us that we should show up for everything in a new state, which we should give a name. If our intensity was measured on a scale of one to ten, we should be at an eight or nine every time.

He likened the four seasons to attitudes in business. Winter was the most hated time, so it was the best time to strike at our competitors with the mantra, "This is my time, winter is my season, I am a gladiator, I will take massive action, I will not be denied!"

He introduced the concept of having raving fans rather than customers, the ten stages of the life cycle of a business, and the concept of optimization—or making incremental improvements in your business processes by just 1 percent which, added together, could equal more than 10 percent. This was so much more manageable and easier to demand than a 10 percent improvement in the company overall.

Then he yelled, "Everybody stand up!" We all stood.

"All those who have been in business for a year, sit down." Many sat down.

"Sit down if you've been in business for two to five years." Many sat down.

"Between six and ten years."

And on he went until he got to, "More than thirty years."

I was still standing. I looked around and saw that I was the only person in that huge hall who was still on my feet. I had the oldest business there.

"What do you do, sir?" asked Tony.

"Barcode solutions," I told him, and he congratulated me. He said I was one of .008 percent of all companies that survived that long.

After this experience, I signed up on the spot for his Business Mastery four-day course, which was amazing. Armed with these tools, I travelled to each of my JVs and trained them for a day in these high-impact techniques.

I was so impressed with his Business Mastery 1 course that I was quite tempted to sign up for Business Mastery 2, but it was in Fiji—half a world away! The course was held at Tony Robbins's retreat center, Namale, where he also lives much of the year. The cost was $10,000, and that was before the airfare and hotel costs. It was a hefty price tag. On the other hand, why not? "Who dares, wins," as they say!

I asked all the JVs if anyone wanted to come with me to split the costs because I was offered two tickets to the course for the price of one. Bless him, Zoltan from Hungary decided to come. Zoltan has always been the first to experiment with all the new business tools I trained them in, so it was no surprise that he wanted to come.

Because Fiji was so far away, it seemed like the perfect opportunity to plan a trip around the world with my second wife, Lisa. We flew from London to San Francisco, to Auckland, to Queenstown, to Wellington, and back to Auckland; then to Fiji, Hong Kong, and Shanghai, where we stayed for a week, so I could conduct my Chinese business.

There must have been about fifty of us at Business Mastery 2. Most were from Australia and New Zealand, the nearest countries, but there was also a smattering of Europeans, all mainly young people with businesses under £1 million. Tony focused on how to make a breakthrough with your business and with your personal life, and we all lapped it up—interspersed every hour or so with rock music and dancing on chairs to loosen us up.

At the beginning, he told us that at the end of the four days, we would have a challenge. We'd be taken to a place where we'd stand on a bridge that was about fifty feet high. From there, we'd jump into the river and float down to a lake. Tony likes challenges. In his "Unleash the Power Within" event he has you walk barefoot on hot coals! This was the Business Mastery equivalent, which he referred to on and off for the four days, which stoked up the anticipation—for some, excitement; for others, wariness and trepidation.

The last night finally came, and around midnight we went to the garden to choose our life jackets and to select a buddy to jump with. We had to jump with a buddy in case either of us got into difficulty, which just added to our wariness. I chose a super chap from Japan whom I'd sat next to for four days. We'd become friends.

We were loaded onto color-coded buses that matched the color of our life jackets, so we could jump in the correct order. It was a long drive. It was pitch black outside, and there were no street lights. We drove deeper and deeper into the interior of the island, and we all wondered how high a fifty-foot bridge would look in the black of night.

We finally arrived and exited the bus but could see nothing. We followed our leader, single-file, until we arrived at the bridge. Through the darkness we could hear the shrieks and splashes of those who'd already jumped. As we got nearer, they gave us head lamps, and then we could see the others as they held hands and jumped.

What a relief! The bridge was, in fact, only about ten feet high. Tony had exaggerated to terrify us, which meant that the relief made the jump all the more delightful. The splash didn't hurt at all, and my buddy and I lay back as we drifted, swept on by the current and fending off the bank with our feet. There was absolutely no sound at all and little light.

I lay on my back for about twenty minutes and gazed at the black sky pinpointed with shiny, twinkling stars. I felt so peaceful that I simply contemplated life in my own bubble, and by the time we reached the lake, I felt completely disconnected from the entire world. We rounded a corner and saw the bobbing lights of boats that were there to pick us up and take us back to the buses. This was disappointing as I could have stayed in that state forever!

We got out of the boats, took off our life jackets, and accepted a goody bag of snacks while we waited for the bus to take us back to the resort. A buzz of excited chatter mounted as we exchanged our experiences with one another, an outgrowth of our pent-up fears and released energy. We reveled in our triumph of facing a fear and conquering it. Even though the jump wasn't a big deal, the buildup certainly had been!

LESSONS LEARNED:

- Push the envelope in your quest for knowledge. The more business skills you have, the better you'll perform and the better you'll be able to teach and motivate others. You can never stop learning. Try to learn in a fun environment. Be trained by the best, face your fears, and do it anyway.

- Look up the tools and contact details at the end of this book and learn from them. These resources will put you way ahead of your competition.

- Tony Robbins says that the biggest mistake most organizations make is to fall in love with their business or products and not with their customers. To take them from being customers to *raving fans*, you need to hammer home the new term to all your staff, so they always think about how to go that extra mile in relationships and service. Make yourself indispensable to the customer and turn them into raving fans!

- Get a team together for a brainstorming session. Choose an in-house process, such as the steps you go through from lead generation to closing a sale. Ask what would happen if you added 20 percent more leads into the sales funnel. How much incremental increase could each person add to each step if they set their mind to it? Then multiply all those increases through to the close, and you'll enjoy an exponential increase in sales.

QUESTIONS FOR YOU:

- Are you in love with your customers?

- How can you turn them into raving fans?

- How can you get an exponential increase in your sales by making incremental improvements to each process in the value chain?

14 RAISING AWARENESS IN GOVERNMENT AND BEYOND

I n the 1990's, I was very involved in all the different AIM Trade Associations: AIM UK, AIM Europe, and AIM International. The barcode industry was still in its infancy; in fact, most countries with AIM affiliates had less than a hundred members who supplied scanners, hand held terminals, printers, and labels. Apart from the manufacturers of hardware, most turned over less than £2m; some would say it was a cottage industry. There was a great need to raise awareness about the benefits of barcodes and to overcome the natural resistance of IT managers, who were scared of anything new that might threaten their jobs if things went wrong.

THE FAR EAST

In 1991, I was president of AIM Europe and was invited to set up the first Scan China in Beijing, so I went to China for the occasion. I was not only keen to expand my horizons in Eastern

Europe; I had an appetite to do so in China as well, so I seized the opportunity to go to search out a joint-venture partner.

The exhibition was very small—mainly a tabletop event—and I needed to create a couple of banners to show what we did. The banners needed to be in Chinese, so I had to get everything translated and printed in Chinese. AIM organized the exhibition and offered a translator, who spent two days at my stand to interpret questions and answers.

I was very excited to visit Beijing, where we stayed at a huge international hotel with the other delegates. The exhibition attracted a number of government ministers who saw the technology as important for the Chinese economy. All the exhibitors lined up on stage and were presented to the minister for commerce and were given beautiful flowers and sashes from some attractive Chinese ladies.

However, the downside was the food! I dislike Chinese food and am, in fact, extremely afraid of it. You never know what sort of animal parts might make up a dish. One lunchtime, we went to a restaurant that had a large glass tank filled with water in which something that looked like a snake twisted and turned. Suddenly, we heard a loud noise and splash. Whatever that creature was, it fell out of the tank and onto the floor. It was immediately set upon by sundry waiters, who chattered excitedly in their high-pitched voices as they tried to wrestle the thing back into its tank without being bitten. That creature was actually on the menu!

On another occasion, the government invited us out to the famous Peking Duck restaurant, which, as the name suggests, serves only duck—not one of my favorite dishes. As president of AIM Europe, I was seated at the top table with the minister. An interpreter sat next to me. Ten of us sat at a round table with a lazy Susan in the middle. The tray had various small dishes in the middle, and we helped ourselves and then let the next person turn it around to select their dishes. I turned to my interpreter and said, "Please explain what each dish is."

"This one is duck intestines, this one is duck feet, and this one is duck brain," he offered.

"Just stop there," I said, as I turned various shades of white and green. "I cannot eat any of these dishes and would rather die than eat any of them." I didn't actually say the last bit, but I made it clear that I would not indulge in these "delicacies."

"You have to show respect to your hosts," the interpreter said, "and eat everything."

You are joking! I thought, but I hatched up a plan to get out of it. I said I wasn't feeling very well and that although everything looked delicious, I was too unwell to eat. Fortunately, he went along with this fib, and I more or less got away with eating just the things I could stomach.

The whole week we spent in Beijing was a bit like this when it came to food until joy of joys, three days before the end of our trip, the first Hard Rock Cafe in China opened. It was just a short walk from my hotel. I and my like-minded colleagues made a beeline for it on the first night and reveled in the delicious hamburgers and chips, and we went back again the next two nights. I was saved! I had lost nearly five pounds during this week.

On the business front, I attracted a lot of interest from delegates and earmarked three possible partners. I visited them after the show and forged some good relationships. But on returning to England, I started to think that barcode adoption in China was years away and that a joint venture now, however seductive, was probably too soon.

How right I was! It was fifteen more years until I returned to China and set up BCS China. In 2006, I was introduced to a young Chinese graduate from the University of Leeds who impressed me. He had started his own small business in computer systems. I visited him in Shanghai and agreed to start a joint venture with him about three years later when I could give it the focus.

I decided to target the supply chain as it was very fragmented in China. There was no carrier that operated nationally. Everything had to be unloaded and offloaded to different carriers to complete its journey, and food was transported without refrigeration. This gave us a perfect opportunity to offer a barcode solution to tackle the problems. The Chinese saw the value in RFID (radio-frequency identification), so we focused on that in addition to barcodes.

What is interesting—and a warning to any who want to set up a business in China—is that they all lie. In fact, it's part of their culture. From a chance remark made by one of my salesmen, I learned that my JV partner had told him that he only needed to work one day a week but that I would pay him for the entire week. Further, my partner told the salesman that because I didn't know about this, he should give the rest of his salary to my JV partner. This went on for over a year without my knowledge, but it explained why I got no sales in that period and had a very small pipeline. After all, I had a salesman who worked only one day per week!

I had it out with my partner, who agreed to give back his shares, and we never spoke again. I found another partner, but this time I didn't give away any shares.

LOBBYING THE GOVERNMENT

Around that time, I noticed several companies that specialized in lobbying the UK government on behalf of their clients who sought to advance their agendas. It seemed to me that with AIM behind me to give credibility, I could do the same to raise awareness about the barcode industry in Parliament.

To this end, I formed the AIM UK Parliamentary Advisory Committee and made a plan to bombard Parliament with stories of how we could help UK companies prosper for the benefit of our members—which would, at the same time, give the association a unique selling point to attract new members.

But first we needed to gain access to ministers, which meant we needed someone on the inside who knew the right people and who could arrange meetings. At the time there was an organization called PITCOM (Parliamentary Information Technology Committee), which was a good place to start. Simon Coombs was the treasurer.

I approached Simon to see if he would be our lobbyist in Parliament and arrange meetings, which he agreed to do. The way to meet most ministers was through their personal private secretaries, and I thus got to meet with the secretary of state for health, one of the home office ministers, and the secretary of the Board of Trade, as it was called then.

We also exhibited at the Tory Party Conference, for which I sold a barcoded access control system to the Dorset Police, which was in charge of security for the occasion. Through Simon and his connections, we got to have our stand on the prime minister's route and we just dared hope that he would visit us. Not only did John Major, the prime minister, visit us, but I was also able to chat with him about barcodes for around three minutes and have my picture taken with him with the AIM UK logo in the background. To crown it all, Home Secretary Michael Howard also came to our stand, and I was able to demonstrate a new two-dimensional barcode that could capture digital photos and signatures. He had a vision to issue barcoded ID cards for each citizen, and this technology would have been perfect for the job. Sadly, his idea subsequently got blown out of the water.

All this lobbying was the catalyst for the Department of Trade and Industry to publish a chapter about barcodes in their monthly magazine for industry, and things took off from there. It was the first time that government literature had mentioned barcodes.

What struck me most was how easy it was to lobby ministers and to ask the prime minister a question in the House of Commons. I got Simon Coombs to ask the prime minister if there was any plan to introduce barcodes on government tenders. It's amazing what you can achieve if you set your mind to it.

EDUCATING THE PUBLIC

We not only needed to raise awareness of our industry with the government; we also needed to attract new people as it was all so new, and it was quite difficult to find new employees who had barcode experience. Since the industry was only about fifteen years old, it was unlikely that anyone younger than twenty would qualify. So I set up an Education Committee at AIM UK, which focused on getting automatic identification, the generic name for the industry, into the school curriculum.

I also chaired the AIM UK membership committee and received an enquiry from Dr. Anthony Furness, who was a tutor at Keele University, based in Stoke in the north of England. Stoke was over a two-hour drive from London, but when I called Dr. Furness, he sounded quite serious. Since I was focused on education, it seemed like getting in the car to go see him was the right thing to do.

This was my first visit to Keele University, and I was impressed by its buildings and heritage, which went back to 1962. However, the original estate was founded in the mid-sixteenth century.

Dr. Furness greeted me with great warmth and looked every bit a professor: grey hair, late forties, glasses, ruddy complexion, and an eager voice.

"Come in and sit down," he said. "Would you like some tea?"

He was very interested in barcodes and wanted to know more about them. He saw the immediate value to business in terms of inventory accuracy by eliminating errors caused by manual inputs. I warmed to him immediately because he was so enthusiastic and couldn't wait to get involved. We talked about what we could do together, and over several meetings we agreed to have Keele University be the center of our education initiative.

Our first project was a laboratory, which was a huge room for AIM members to showcase their equipment and solutions. There was a big rush to donate or lend equipment to the laboratory, which was there so that customers could visit and try the various barcoding solutions. In addition, we started a distance-learning course that Dr. Furness wrote and the world's first master of science degree in automatic identification technology, which was delivered in the AIM laboratory. This was how we taught students the benefits of barcodes and encouraged them to go into the industry as a career.

It was a great success and lasted a few years until Tony left and joined AIM UK as technical director. He became our first professor in automatic identification, having written several research papers and given many lectures on the subject. He carried on his evangelical work for the industry over the next several years.

LESSONS LEARNED:

- Think big. Who would have thought that I would have a personal conversation with the prime minister?

- Focus and achieve.

- Be a philanthropist. Think of ways you can promote your industry/company by serving others and expanding knowledge which, in turn, enhances your credibility and grows your stature and reputation.

- It's often difficult to kick-start a market in a new technology, so be evangelical about it. Use blogs and social media, and promote white papers on your website—tools we never had in those days. You can also pay key influencers to raise awareness among their followers and networks, so it's important to identify who they are and feed them a constant diet of use cases to get the word out to the mainstream.

QUESTIONS FOR YOU:

- How do you think the government could help you grow your business?

- Do you and your company have a strong reputation in the market?

- Is your offering new and disruptive, or are you just recycling existing ideas to do it better than others?

- Who are the influencers in your market?

- What material could you provide market influencers to connect with their followers?

15 *WHEN THINGS GO WRONG*

At one of our staff dinners, I sat next to Cathy, who ran our Film Master business. She'd worked with us for about four years and was having difficulties at home. Her grandmother was ill. Liz spent a lot of time with Cathy, who was quite young—in her twenties at the time. She counseled her and talked her through her troubles. At the dinner, Cathy told me how wonderful Liz and I had been to her and how grateful she was—so much so that she considered us family. This touched us; it was nice to know that our genuine efforts to create a family atmosphere at Bar Code Systems had borne fruit.

Three weeks later, Cathy came into my office and handed in her notice. She wouldn't say why. I was stunned, based on what she'd said a few weeks ago. The following week, I learned that Cathy

I learned that Cathy had left to start her own Film Master business and that she had taken a copy of my customer base with her.

had left to start her own Film Master business and that she had taken a copy of my customer base with her.

I felt like a dagger had been plunged in my heart. How could someone do something like that? I felt totally betrayed and wondered if I could trust anyone again. Cathy was a brilliant employee and had played a huge role in the growth of our Film Master business. She was the BCS face to the customer and the first voice they heard when they phoned in. Our relationship had seemed great, so it took me a long time to grasp that this had actually happened. It seemed like a bad dream.

I immediately ordered new security for the computers so that nobody else could steal my customers. The only way to stop someone else from doing this was to deny them access, but then how could they do their jobs properly?

I will never know how much damage Cathy did because our sales continued to grow over the next few years; but I figure it cost me about £75,000 in lost profits. I don't know what happened to Cathy, but deep inside me I feel that most of our customers wouldn't condone such actions. It just encourages other people to do the same thing, and they could well be the next victim.

FURTHER BETRAYAL

I invested a fair amount of money and hired some salesmen to sell systems and some engineers to put them together. In 1992, our sales reached the £2 million mark. Sales grew over the next two years, thanks in great part to the Logistics exhibitions on the Oriana ship. But profits started to drop. Thanks to the print services division, which consisted of the Film Masters, verifiers, printers, and labels—and especially the label bureau—we still turned a profit, but in the systems area, we were losing money at an alarming rate. It would take six to nine months to get our first order and probably another three months to deliver it. This would crush our cash flow.

Toward the end of 1995, when my Film Master business started to degrade because of Macbarcoda, the software that generated barcode artwork directly on plate-ready film, and my systems sales started to take off, four key members of my staff— my technical manager, system salesman, systems manager, and business development manager for the JVs—marched into my office.

"We don't like the way you're running the company," they said. Mutiny!

"So you run it," I said.

"Well, actually, we're all leaving to set up our own business in the systems market, and we're taking your best customer, Entertainment UK, with us."

> *"Well, actually, we're all leaving to set up our own business in the systems market, and we're taking your best customer, Entertainment UK, with us."*

How was that for loyalty? Most of them had worked for me for ten years. The company wasn't in great shape, and this was certainly not going to improve things, but I told them to get out. I didn't want them to have the opportunity to steal my customer base like Cathy had done, but in truth, they'd probably already done so.

The next year I grew the sales team again, but I took a revenue hit over the next two years and started hemorrhaging profits. So I got rid of most of them and started to look around for alternatives again.

One winter day in 1998, I was on the ski slopes in the French Alps and got a phone call. I came to a halt and wrestled my phone out of the pocket of my ski jacket.

"Hi, Brian," a voice said. "Hope I'm not disturbing you." It was the country manager of Symbol Technologies UK, my main scanner hardware supplier.

"No, not at all," I said hastily, as I tried to gain my composure. "I'm out skiing in the Alps."

"Sorry to disturb you," he said, "but I wonder if you could come into the office when you get back. I have something important to discuss with you."

"Sure. I look forward to it."

I wondered what on earth this could be about. He'd never called me before, and although we had a good, professional business arrangement, I'd never been summoned to meet him. I couldn't imagine what was so important that he wanted to discuss with me, but I had a little frisson of excitement and anticipation that made the rest of my holiday a bit more thrilling.

I went to see him on my return, and after the usual pleasantries and small talk, he said, "Look, Brian, you probably know that a couple of years ago we started to sell systems solutions ourselves."

I did know that and was not pleased that they were in direct competition with us.

"Well," he went on, "I'm not happy with the way things are going and want to get rid of the division. I thought Bar Code Systems might like to take it over. It's managed by a good chap, and if you can persuade him, I'm sure he would come to work for you."

You could have knocked me over with a feather! I couldn't believe my luck. It was like all my Christmases had come at once. I was so delighted I could barely contain myself. In fact, I almost got up and kissed him! I was extremely grateful for the opportunity and said as much.

Their revenue was around £2 million, and they had a good base of customers. As far as having a manager for our own systems division, I hadn't yet worked that out. I knew I wasn't the right person to run it. Maybe this guy could be an answer sent from heaven.

I called Steve right away to see if he might be interested in the job. He wasn't happy that he'd been given the boot, although it was ameliorated a bit by the opportunity to rise and shine at BCS. He took some persuading, but perhaps that was a negotiating tactic because he ultimately got an £80,000 salary, plus his accommodation during the week. He planned to stay in the city during the week and commute from his home, which was over two hours away.

This was a great deal more than I'd paid anyone before. He took a while to accept my offer, but Steve finally did and started almost immediately.

And then a funny thing happened. My contact at Symbol Technologies who'd offered me the deal changed his mind. He decided not to give *all* the customers to me. He was going to keep the good ones and continue to service them, and I'd get the duds.

> *My contact at Symbol Technologies who'd offered me the deal changed his mind. He decided not to give all the customers to me.*

I was incensed. In one day, I'd gone from visualizing an extra £2 million in sales, which would double our revenue almost overnight, to being stuck with some smaller customers that I'd have to nurture and grow. And I now had Steve, a very expensive managing director whose salary I could no longer justify. But I decided to give it a go. We had Steve and a new sales team in place, and our plan was good—a plan that focused on custom software.

But over the next two years, sales hardly grew. Then disaster struck again.

LOSSES

In 2000, we lost £150,000 on revenue of £1.8 million, which was much lower than the previous year. Steve did not perform at all. He had no idea how to manage a company, let alone sell systems. One of my salesmen resigned and then came back, another underperformed, and no one on the team ever embraced the custom software idea; so everyone was demotivated.

I kicked Steve out and took the helm myself. I worked on a new strategy to build out-of-the-box software for the transportation market and went on another Logistics exhibition cruise.

I managed to get buy-in from the staff, and things started to improve; but we still didn't meet critical mass in systems, which is what we needed.

My strategy was good for 2001, so I hired a systems man who used to work for Symbol. He was very expensive, as were all Symbol employees! The reason I could afford him was that the profits from our labels, printers, and verifiers business could finance his hire. Three months later, I took him with me to meet the new corporate banker who'd taken over our account. The banker immediately asked both of us for personal guarantees, which caused my new hire to resign even before he started! I signed the guarantees; I had faith in the company.

But without this new hire, I couldn't execute my strategy, and I needed to cut costs. I trimmed the budget by £1 million by eliminating redundancies and decided to divest myself of the systems business, which was dragging us down. But I had some great customers that had bought our custom software, and I couldn't leave them in the lurch because their operations would have ground to a halt.

My great friend Tim Hankins came to my rescue. He'd been instrumental in developing our RFID business, and I passed my systems division over to his company for 50 percent of the gross margins on any deals. He agreed to service my existing software customers, and by February 2002 prospects looked quite good.

But the bank became more nervous, and they called in an insolvency firm to produce a statement of affairs. It was highly inaccurate—and caused me to liquidate Bar Code Systems, as explained in chapter 8.

LESSONS LEARNED:

- You must lock your key staff into an employment contract that has a noncompete clause. It may not be forever but will be a deterrent, and having one would have stopped me from losing one of my key staff.

- Like Tony Robbins taught me, you must show up with at least an eight-level intensity every day. If you have good staff, they'll test you and judge you and be ready to pounce on your weaknesses. I lost the respect of the senior systems team because they didn't believe in my vision. I had let things slide and my performance had slipped. Don't let that happen to you.

- Have a plan B. Things often go wrong, so you must have a fallback plan. You must be proactive. Back then, I was reactive and didn't have an alternate vision to motivate and retain my team.

QUESTIONS FOR YOU:

- Does your key staff have employment contracts?

- Do they include a fair noncompete clause?

- How are you being proactive to retain the respect of your team?

- Do you have a plan B?

16 *RISE AGAIN!*

The year 2002 was horrible. I had to come up with a plan that didn't include systems solutions. I'd tried to make it work before, but I had failed for three reasons:

- We were ahead of our time. The market wasn't ready to pivot from purchasing hardware to purchasing total solutions.

- Our sales were inconsistent and unpredictable, which invalidated our cash-flow forecasts.

- We were undercapitalized, and the Film Master business was dying off, so my former cash cow could no longer pay the essential bills.

Bar Code Systems UK Ltd had folded, but Bar Code Systems (London) was still a going concern. I had formed BCS London after the Axis acquisition so I could track their old customers. I was paying the previous owner a commission on the continued sales from his customers, and it was easiest to put them all into a new entity. BCS London sold print services, Film Masters, printers, labels, label bureau, and verifiers. We focused on retailers and their suppliers, which took us back to first base and our core business. Once again, our purpose was to take the mystique out of barcodes and achieve a first-time scan at the checkout.

We also changed the financial structure so that International Bar Code Systems (IBCS) and BCS London operated independently and neither division could bring down the other.

We moved our offices to an industrial site near Heathrow Airport and hired a young sales staff, a new marketing manager, and a label salesman who'd been in the business for years. Project Phoenix was up and running.

As it turned out, 2002 was also a terrible year for IBCS. I had arranged for all the JVs to purchase product from my main suppliers through the original Bar Code Systems, which I then sold at a 15 percent markup. This was great business for me, and it helped them because nobody wanted to give credit to Eastern Europe, even though their custom was to pay on delivery. At that time, credit was unheard of, and everything was done on a cash basis.

Hence, I could only get a £100,000 line of credit for IBCS and £400,000 for BCS London, which I had formerly used to finance IBCS. Now I could no longer do that.

This arrangement worked just fine until we started to sell more and more to the JVs. But the more we sold, the more cash I had to come up with to finance the bigger and bigger deals. Then some Eastern European customers got familiar with using credit and took longer than ever to pay, particularly Russia, which stretched me to breaking point.

So when the bank kicked us out and I was unable to get overdraft privileges, I changed the business model for IBCS. I put them in touch with Symbol and Zebra, our two key suppliers, so they could buy direct from them. But this left a big hole in our profits. We sold £15 million of goods to the JVs, but now

I no longer got the 15 percent commission. I decided to charge them a monthly service fee instead, which they agreed to pay.

BACK TO LIZ

Liz, thank goodness, came back to work in the company. She'd taken a break to raise Jessica when we first adopted and had come back for a couple of years but then left again because she couldn't stand working with me. In the few years when we were still small, everything had been very relaxed; but as time passed, I became more stressed and experienced more and more problems, which I took out on her. Later, when she saw that the company was in trouble, she agreed to come back again, and I agreed to be on my best behavior. It worked.

But her cancer had returned, and it spread to the liver. On one of our regular visits to the hospital, the doctor examined her behind a screen and read her X-ray. He gave me a look that told me everything, and I knew that my darling Liz was now on borrowed time.

She fought breast cancer for ten years, during which she tried thirty treatments, mostly natural. I became an expert on breast cancer and on handling women. She taught me that women don't like to be fixed and when they pour out their problems, all a man has to do is just listen and nod his head. Even while she was sick, Liz always looked great, which annoyed her because people didn't understand how ill she truly was.

Liz was back at the company when she took a turn for the worse, and we made many hospital visits to have the liquid drained from her lungs. In August 2004, I'd paid an exorbitant amount for the three of us to go to the Olympics in Athens. We wanted Jess, now thirteen, to see the gymnastics, as she was becoming a great gymnast. One of Liz's hospital stays clashed with the Olympics, and she couldn't go—but she insisted that Jess and I go without her. And we did. But it was to my profound regret that we did so because Liz passed away three weeks after we got back. Awash in sorrow, all I could think about was that I could have spent that time with her.

RESTRUCTURING

In 2005, all was well in BCS London and IBCS, which were both now part of one of Symbol's many partner affiliate programs. Symbol employed a company, JS Group based in New Jersey, to deliver part of the program—an audit of our sales team and recommendations about how to grow them. I had seen JS Group make presentations at some of Symbol's functions and was very impressed with them. They specialized in helping channel partners grow to the next level, and they understood our mobility marketplace.

An idea started to gel in my mind. I wondered if I could get the JVs to pay for JS Group to work on a plan for us. I had identified a shift in the market and was thinking about how we should structure ourselves to grow to the next level.

I visited JS Group in the States to see what they could do for us and spent a couple days briefing their team on our situation and our history. At the time, the entire technology channel was in the midst of a transformation from product-centric sales to consultative sales, and they felt like they could come up with a plan to help us address that. The cost would be $20,000, which I thought was very reasonable, especially when we managed to persuade Symbol to pay for it out of marketing development funds.

The solution was to change from a hardware sales company, which made up 84 percent of our revenue, to a mix of 40 percent hardware, 30 percent software, and 30 percent services. They compared this model to what they and IBM called an application solution integrator, or ASI. I'd never heard this term before, but it made sense and sounded good to me.

To make this transformation, we had to invest a great deal of money to purchase more hardware, hire software engineers, and build a customer-service department and help desk. In some cases, we offered a twenty-four-hour help desk at a premium price for our customers for whom our solution became mission critical.

We used these ratios of hardware: services/software as our main KPIs. They were a great driver and benchmark then, and we use them to this day. The plan to become an ASI made perfect sense since margins on hardware were going down dramatically. We needed more profitable products and, at the same time, needed to erect more barriers for our competitors.

———

Our sales team had to become more consultative, so we hired a company to talk us through the QUIS methodology. Many of our salespeople needed to change their entire approach, and this new sales method took them out of their comfort zone. It was hard at first, and they often approached a customer to sell them their latest and greatest box, when they should have asked him about the three things kept him awake at night, in order to gain insights into their real needs and figure out if there was a fit.

If there wasn't a fit, then we could still come away with something. I told the sales team to get at least one or two referrals before they left the customer. If they were calling on current customers, it should be even easier to get referrals because by then we should be their trusted advisor.

We had to let many of our salespeople go because they couldn't make the change. We hired other salespeople who had consultative sales experience or who could adapt.

We started to write our own software, such as asset management, traceability, and warehouse management software. Although I couldn't make systems work for BCS years earlier, this new approach from JS Group gave us a great strategy for the JVs, and services became the highest-margin part of our business.

But at first it represented a learning curve for our customers. Customers expected to pay nothing for services, such as training, for example. I taught our sales team if they gave a service for free, it would have no value in the customer's eyes. We had to assign a value to each type of service and then sell that value to obtain our price. Anyone could provide a service for nothing, and some competitors used free services to beat us in a deal; but we built up a reputation of providing solutions that always worked, so why jeopardize something mission critical for the sake of one free service?

As customers became savvier, we developed more sophisticated services. For example, we staged their solution prior to delivery so that the latest software version was installed on their handheld terminals. They got a printed inventory of everything in the box—including the accessories. We installed their wireless infrastructure after site surveys and presented them with an out-of-the-box solution for which we charged a premium. Sometimes this even included a six-month "health check" to make sure everything was still operating at optimum level. Our goal was to make ourselves so indispensable that we became their trusted advisors and they'd ask us to sit on their technology committees to plan their roadmap for the next three years.

No doubt, without the JS Group we would still be selling boxes at ever-decreasing margins. In fact, we'd most likely be bankrupt instead of being market leaders.

LESSONS LEARNED:

- As CEO, you must always have the big picture in mind so that you can see far enough into the future to anticipate changes in the market and stay ahead of your competitors. Our approach was to change our business model every three years or so, which raised the barriers to market entry as much as possible.

Sometimes that required a culture shift, and I had to let some staff go who couldn't adapt. It was sad, but we lost a few of our stars as a result of this.

- Consultants are expensive, but I found that JS Group could look at my business dispassionately and come up with a great plan that would take us to the next level. I'd never heard of an ASI, and even now I don't think many people outside our group know what I am talking about. But those KPIs of 40 percent hardware and 30 percent each of software and services kept us on track.

- If you have a plan that works, don't listen to other people when they want to point you in a different direction. Believe in yourself and see it through to the end.

- Be bold with customers. Don't shy away. Make them pay for things that have value and charge them a lot for the privilege.

QUESTIONS FOR YOU:

- How long do you think your current business model will continue to add value?

- Do you have a vision to change it?

- Are you bold enough to do it?

- Think back to a time when you hired a consultant. Was it a profitable move? What was the gain? Would you hire one again?

- Are you bold enough to increase your prices and charge for services? Are you afraid you'll lose customers? Is there something you could offer them in return?

17 *SPOT THE NEXT TREND*

I've always liked to be at the cutting edge of technology, and we were quick to change our business model to keep up with the latest tech developments. We have led the way. The goal was to always make it harder for our competitors to beat us in any deal, and for that we had to raise the bar.

I always wanted Bar Code Systems to be an experimental bed for the joint ventures. I calculated that Eastern Europe was about three years behind Western Europe and the States. It was, therefore, quite easy to predict what would happen over there, provided I kept my eye on technology coming from the States. This was the main reason for me to be involved with AIM for so long and for my visits to Eastern Europe for industry exhibitions.

Success comes when you can spot the next trend or adapt to difficulties created when serious problems happen in your company.

Success comes when you can spot the next trend or adapt to difficulties created when serious problems happen in your company.

Although I've often relied on my gut, when I weighed the alternative routes, I was actually connecting the dots. I would be unable to explain this had my hero Steve Jobs of Apple fame not given his famous Stanford Commencement Speech in June 2005.

He told three stories. The first was called "Connecting the Dots." He talked about how when he left college, he started noticing labels and banners that had beautiful hand calligraphy; so he decided that in his free time, he would attend a course. This is where he learned about typefaces and how they used variable spaces. Ten years later when he was designing the first Macintosh computer, he remembered this course and designed all the fonts to have smooth outlines and proportionate spaces between the characters. Windows copied him, and thus all computers have beautiful fonts, which would never have happened had he not taken a calligraphy course.

As he said, "You can't connect the dots looking forward. You can only connect them looking backward. So you have to trust that the dots will somehow connect in your future. You have to trust in something—your gut, destiny, life, karma, whatever. Because believing that the dots will connect down the road will give you the confidence to follow your heart, even when it leads you off the well-worn path. And that will make all the difference."

As Lewis Carroll wrote in *Alice in Wonderland*:

> Cat: "Where are you going?"
> Alice: "Which way should I go?"
> Cat: "That depends on where you are going."
> Alice: "I don't know."
> Cat: "Then it doesn't matter which way you go."

CONNECT THE DOTS

When I was in the German Embassy and found the brochure about Film Masters, I connected the dots: barcodes, printing paper, printers. I felt that glasnost and perestroika would lead to the fall of the Berlin Wall and open up new markets for barcodes, which would free me from Symbol's direct sales force.

When I worked for Jack Hickman and he took me to Europe to sell the idea of a total solution in barcodes, he was ahead of his time. When JS Group presented similar ideas to Symbol fifteen years later, I knew it was the time for total solutions.

When I read about Desert Storm and the problems they were having with blood bags—and had just learned about PDF 417—I connected the dots and knew that PDF was the solution.

Now I've connected that a barcode is just a sensor, as is an RFID chip, and they both can be harnessed to collect data 24/7. As such, it's a part of the ecosystem that is the Internet of Things. I'm also connecting the dots that the blockchain or equivalent will provide a decentralized, immutable ledger that will disrupt the supply chain and the whole financial edifice. Banks beware! I am convinced we can be part of this and add value for our customers. I just have to find a way to make it work in *our* solutions.

What I'm saying is that you have to keep the big picture in mind, all the time. If I had focused only on a small part of the market and our position in it, I wouldn't have seen the bigger opportunities.

> **You have to keep the big picture in mind, all the time.**

It's the legendary story about the three stonecutters:

One day a traveler, walking along a lane, came across three stonecutters working in a quarry. Each was busy cutting a block of stone. Interested to find out what they were working on, he asked the first stonecutter what he was doing.

"I am cutting a stone!"

Still no wiser, the traveler turned to the second stonecutter and asked him what he was doing.

"I am cutting this block of stone to make sure that it's square and its dimensions are uniform, so that it will fit exactly in its place in a wall."

A bit closer to finding out what the stonecutters were working on, but still unclear, the traveler turned to the third stonecutter. He seemed to be the happiest of the three, and when asked what he was doing, he replied, "I am building a cathedral!"

Connecting the dots is not without risk. Every time I did so, executing my ideas was risky. You must have a risk mindset. I always found it helpful to ask, "What's the worst that can happen if I fail?" The answer was that I'd be back where I started. If I went bust, I could always pick myself up and start over again. I developed a plan B in case things went wrong and could change my strategy if I needed to.

Finally, I asked myself how I'd feel if I didn't go forward. Would I regret it for the rest of my life? One of my many mantras is that I have no regrets at all in life, nor will I ever. Never look *backward*; look *forward*. Have the courage of your convictions and generate your own self-confidence by ticking off goals and achievements. Recognize that failure is good—provided you learn from it— and always remain positive and mix with positive people.

So keep your eyes open, carry the big picture with you, accept data gleaned from everywhere that relates to your business, and dare to think the unthinkable. Trust your gut and follow your heart; keep looking and *don't settle*.

EXPANDING TECHNOLOGIES

Sometimes, however, I found myself up against a wall, such as in the early 1990s when a company called Wherenet burst onto the scene with a new RFID tag that could store a great deal of data. It used three Wi-Fi access points to give the exact location of an object in a large area. For example, in a yard where newly manufactured cars are stored, each specific car could be located. Or in a yard full of containers, a specific container could be located and its contents identified.

This technology is called RTLS, real-time location systems. Although the tags were very expensive, about thirty-five dollars each in those days, I saw a big market in automotive and shipping. In fact, we became a Wherenet partner, but the applications were slow to get traction mainly because of the cost of the tags. A few years ago, Zebra bought Wherenet, which gave me hope that it would kick-start the market; but when I tried to find someone from Zebra in our region who could support us, there was no one.

The same thing happened with a part of Motorola that offered broadband. They had antennas that enhanced the signal so that it could reach almost a hundred kilometres. This would be great for offering broadband in a city or for linking warehouses together that were a long distance from each other. But once again, we got no support and ended up with just one customer who wanted to connect three warehouses in Poland.

My latest technological venture is the Internet of Things (IoT)—or Internet of Everything, as some like to call it—where sensors that are connected to the Internet through broadband, Wi-Fi, or the mobile networks, transmit continuous data that can be collected by applications, so the customer can make business decisions in real time. It's forecast that by 2020, there will be fifty billion sensors connected to all sorts of devices like toothbrushes, washing machines, cars, water meters, lamp posts—pretty much anything. This will turn them into *smart* products, and they'll all talk to the Internet and to each other continuously. And they'll generate a large amount of data. To provide an IoT solution, one needs an ecosystem of partners to provide the sensors, infrastructure, gateway to the Internet, data analytics, business application software, and all the services around these. Enormous opportunity.

For us, it's an extension of what we do now. We understand how these technologies work and how to provide a solution. But there are so many applications that could use the Internet of Things that we need to focus on just one or two. We must learn enough about them to become experts and trusted advisors and to find the right partners for our ecosystem.

At the moment, there are no less than 461 IoT platforms that enable sensors to transmit data via the Internet and through to the ultimate business application. Zebra has developed one of these platforms, called Savannah, and they use it amongst other things, to remotely control their printers and to count the labels printed. Thus, they can monitor label usage and replenish them with blank labels and ribbons *before* the customer runs out of stock. Nice idea.

I like this predictive approach to things. If you can predict when a machine is likely to break down, you can send spare parts or an engineer in advance, so there's no downtime at the factory. It could apply to elevators or anything else that needs maintenance. It can also apply to humans, say, dementia patients, as general practitioners are inundated with appointments from sufferers to check up on them to make sure they don't get worse, but if the patient wore sensors which monitored their blood pressure, pulse, what sort of sleep quality they got, if they took their medicine regularly and all sorts of other things, then they can call the patient in for a review and reduce their appointment load and free up valuable appointments for those in real need.

INTERNET OF THINGS

We're trying to find some tame customers to run a no-cost proof of concept, so we can develop some great solutions. It's unlikely that the company would have an IoT strategy, and they may even be unaware of the benefits IoT can offer. They could fear they would lose their jobs if the system doesn't work, which is why we'll offer the first proof of concept free of charge.

Predictive maintenance is the first project on our development list, followed by logistics. Our vision is to put an RFID tag on a parcel that will monitor the temperature and register any sharp knocks the package has en route. At the moment, courier companies track only the location of a parcel and where it has been at any one time. But if it arrives damaged, they can't trace where the damage happened or who is responsible.

Even in the West, there are not many industrial IoT systems

out there, although the big systems houses are developing some. One area that has traction is smart cities. This is where, for example, a sensor can be placed on a lamp post with the new LED street lights. The volume of light for each lamp post can be controlled individually for the specific time of day, which saves energy. Other sensors can also be fixed to these same lamp posts to determine traffic volume and control the traffic lights. Cities can also monitor water usage with smart meters to save energy. Garbage collection can be reduced by sensing when a bin is full and then sending the truck to collect it when needed, rather than once per week. In London, electronic bus signage relays arrival times at each stop, thanks to sensors along the route. Parking at airports and in shopping malls has improved because some have sensors at each bay that turn on a green light to show that a space is free.

The smart phone has been a catalyst for most of these applications. The data from the sensor is sent to an app on a smart phone, which makes monitoring a simple and portable function. Soon, most software programs will become mobile apps, which we all expect for free.

I actually think smart phones will soon disappear—maybe by 2025—as a new generation of glasses will hit the market that use augmented reality technology. Information from the application will project onto the lenses that will be controlled by hand gestures.

Our best chance of success is to position ourselves as a value-added service provider in IoT. This is similar to our application solution integration model and will fill a gap in the market. We will consult on the best combination of sensor, platform, data analytics, and solution, and will project-manage the partners to provide the integration, services, and support that are needed. That will make us the single point of contact for the customer and will help us gain experience, which will hopefully lead us to develop the killer app we all seek.

And I'm still networking. I go to as many IoT and blockchain conferences as I can to make connections and confirm the validity of our market position. I also look for use cases to give the technology more credibility, while we look for early adopters. In my role as councillor in London, I joined the All Party Parliamentary Group on Smart Cities and attend a lot of functions around this subject, which helps build my knowledge base. I like to think that we are ahead of the competition, and that once more we will be able to lead the pack.

BLOCKCHAIN

There's another new technology, and I'm trying to find ways to incorporate it into our solutions: blockchain. It's the same underlying technology that Bitcoin uses, and so far, it's gotten traction with FinTech (financial technology) applications and banks. Blockchain cuts out the middleman and is faster, cheaper, and more secure than existing transactions, which is why banks are worried they'll become extinct one day.

Here's an overview of how blockchain works. A transaction creates a block, which is placed on the blockchain. The blockchain is a network of computers that, through consensus, registers each transaction and copies it to every network node in the chain. To use conventional banking as an example, the blockchain is like a full history of all transactions, and blocks are like individual bank statements or ledgers. The blockchain is copied to a series of nodes—computers that are connected to the Bitcoin network that validate and relay transactions. Thus, transactions cannot be altered, duplicated, or falsified because everyone with access to the blockchain has visibility. Only the buyer and seller have the electronic key that allows them to create or change the transaction. No one person has sole access to the ledger, which reduces the possibility of fraud. Information about ownership, provenance, authenticity, and price are all held in the blockchain.

Bitcoin and other digital currencies aren't the only applications for blockchain. Digital product memories that are connected to smart devices along the supply chain provide secure proof of everything from provenance to the end user. Blockchain has the potential to become the new gold standard of business and trade; it can help reinforce trust in today's complex and globalized world.

So how can we use it in our business? In the shipping industry, it can replace bills of lading, cumbersome logs, spreadsheets, data intermediaries, and private databases. IoT devices will be connected to blockchain records for instant access and will cut out many third parties. A "smart contract" can be created and triggered automatically when certain conditions are met, without the need for long-winded paper trail and human authorization. For example, when a shipment is received, it can be scanned to trigger the transfer of ownership of the goods and to authorize release of payment. Because the parameters of the contract are encrypted, all parties work off the same contract, which cannot be tampered with.

At the moment, I'm planning to launch our own cryptocurrency called TraceCoin. Our solutions are mainly track and trace solutions. We will have our own blockchain, which our customers will use initially. Each barcode that is generated for an asset will have a fraction of a TraceCoin assigned to it and then registered on our blockchain. Customers will pay TraceCoin to use our blockchain, and the more assets they track and barcodes they scan, they will earn rewards in TraceCoin. Our staff and other stakeholders will also have the opportunity to earn TraceCoins, which can be exchanged for discounts, rewards, or cash.

Our customers will like this system because they will get instant, validated payments from their own customers and will have a more secure and trusted environment for their operations. Ultimately, TraceCoin will have enormous value through usage, and our blockchain will be popular enough to go global rather than regional in Eastern Europe. That is the dream anyway.

This is an area where we can get involved if we incorporate some links to the blockchain databases in our supply-chain software. Maybe by the time you read this, we'll have some installations and maybe even a killer app!

To understand our connected future, all we have to do is dream. Imagine the possibilities of all those sensors located in objects everywhere—a world that offers us a constant stream of data about what is going on around us. Just imagine what we can create from that data and how blockchain or a similar technology will eliminate the middleman and maybe even create a global currency. It's in its early days yet—equivalent to dot com in the 1990s with Netscape and CompuServe. The Googles and Facebooks and Amazons of the crypto world haven't yet been invented. What if Facebook with its 2.5 billion users issued its own Facebook coin? It could become the global currency of choice. What new opportunities can you imagine? How can you change the world?

LESSONS LEARNED:

- You must always keep ahead of the competition. If you choose to do this by beating them with all the latest technologies, you must participate in conferences, network with people who are in the know, and read copious articles. Don't be afraid to build a test ecosystem to find out which partners work and which do not. You'll learn a lot from these suppliers who have already achieved some installations.

- At the end of the day, you'll need to connect with some tame customers and offer them a proof of concept. Chances are they won't have an IoT or blockchain strategy, so you'll have to do all the work for them when you try to sell them on the idea. So do some serious market research among your customer base to find the ones who can best benefit from the new technology.

QUESTIONS FOR YOU:

- Do you go to industry conferences and network?

- Have you ever obtained significant business from a conference?

APPENDIX A: HIRING TALENT STRATEGY

BEFORE

If you start the hiring process the moment you have a new vacancy or someone hands in their notice, it is often too late. To build a pipeline ready for when you have a gap, you must continually interview or have informal meetings with standout candidates who have the skills you need.

Have an engaging website that reflects the culture of your business. Post a description of each of your departments and allow candidates to share their CVs or resumes. Use LinkedIn to informally reach out to professionals.

Having a dedicated talent person who takes care of recruitment, HR, and culture has greater benefits than simply managing the hiring process. Such a team member can genuinely save money by ensuring you get the very best person in the market at the right price and with limited impact to the business.

DURING

Have a strategic interview process. Ask yourself what you expect to learn from the interview. Can the candidate perform the role? Are they technical enough? Do they fit in your culture? Do they have hustle and passion? Have a four-stage process consisting of a culture interview, technical interview, test, and social interview.

Ask three important questions:

- Why are you interviewing with us / thinking of leaving your current role? (This can be used in counteroffer situations; it also helps you understand if your goals align.)

- How would your current employer feel about you handing in your notice?

- If I offered you the job today, would you accept it? Anything other than positive responses should be treated mindfully.

THE OFFER

When you extend the offer, be sure to show how excited you are about them and the impact they can make. Create buy-in. Between the time they give notice to their former company and when they actually join yours, invite them to company events or to meet the team for lunch. We send a "new starter pack" in the post with a branded notepad, pen, USB, and a handwritten note from their line manager.

AFTER

During the first couple of weeks, a new employee makes up their mind about their new role and employer. Make their first day as integrated as possible. Have their work station ready on day one, and make plans for them to meet the teams. Weekly one-to-ones for the first month are crucial. If they have a probationary period, meet with them in the middle of that term and at the end, then follow with quarterly one-to-one meetings.

The number-one requirement for millennials (born between 1980 and 1999) is training and development opportunities. The second is flexibility in the workplace.

Having an excellent talent strategy goes wider than just recruiting. It's retention, culture, opportunities, work environment, and progression.

The cost of setting aside a small budget allocated per person, each year (£2,000-£4,000) is usually a much smaller cost than replacing those that are unsatisfied and leave (around £30k).

Thanks to Gemma Bianchi of Greenwood Campbell for sharing this information.

APPENDIX B: INTERVIEW QUESTIONS

QUESTIONS TO REVEAL POTENTIAL FAILURE AREAS:

- What three adjectives best describe your personality?

- Describe a specific situation when your personality or style helped you in your job and another situation when it hindered you.

- How would your subordinates describe you?

- What about your supervisors?

- Why are they different (if they are)?

- Would you have described yourself this way five years ago?

- What type of work do you find least satisfying?

- Give me a relevant example and compare this to the type of work you find most satisfying.

- Everyone has strengths and weaknesses. Openly admitting our weaknesses allows us to grow and is a sign of strength. What's the one critical area that has caused you problems that you'd like to change?

QUESTIONS TO REVEAL TRAITS AND BEHAVIORS IN A SITUATIONAL CONTEXT:

- How important is your career to you? Tell me about a time you had to make a personal sacrifice to achieve a career objective.

- Have you ever been totally motivated, even consumed, by a task or a job? Tell me about it.

QUESTIONS TO REVEAL CHARACTER, VALUES, ESTEEM, AND GOALS:

- There is never enough time to do everything. How do you prioritize what's important to you? Consider family, career, personal growth, and social issues.

- Why do you prioritize these as you do? Have you ever had to make compromises when issues competed with each other?

- How have you improved yourself over the past year? What books have you read?

- Values and character are usually developed early in youth, sometimes as a result of an important family situation—even a crisis. What are some of your important values and how were they formed?

- Tell me about a few significant goals you've already achieved.

- In the last year, have you established any new personal or career goals for yourself? Are they written? How are these progressing?

QUESTION TO DETERMINE PERSUASIVENESS AND ASSERTIVENESS:

- Tell me about a situation that caused you lots of stress—maybe even something that didn't work out as well as you would have liked.

QUESTIONS TO DETERMINE ABILITY TO IMPLEMENT CHANGE, INITIATIVE, AND SELF-MOTIVATION:

- What have you done on your own to improve your skills and abilities over the past few years?

- What was your objective and how satisfied are you with the results?

- Initiative is essential for success in our company. Give me some examples of where you took the initiative and the impact it had.

- What do you want in a job? Why is having this important to you?

QUESTIONS TO DETERMINE APPLICANT INTEREST AND MOTIVATION:

- Describe your ideal company and job. Why are these important to you?

- Why are you looking for a new position?

FORCED-CHOICE QUESTIONS TO DETERMINE COMPETENCY WITHIN A WORK-TYPE:

- How many experiences have you had specifically with handling customer complaints?

- Describe your most extensive involvement in this area and some results of your efforts.

QUESTION TO TEST YOUR OFFER:

- I still need to get official approval before we can extend an offer, but what are your thoughts now about the position?

CLOSING QUESTIONS:

- We don't have all of the feedback yet on you or our other candidates, but I think you'd be one of our finalists if interested.

- How do you feel about the job on a 0-10 scale?

- What issues need to be addressed to get you closer to a 10?

- Is this the type of position that would interest you?

- What do you think you could accomplish if this position were yours? How would you go about this?

APPENDIX C: BOOKS TO READ

The 7 Habits of Highly Effective People by Stephen Covey

Good to Great: Why Some Companies Make the Leap and Others Don't by Jim Collins

Touching the Void: The True Story of One Man's Miraculous Survival by Joe Simpson

The World Is Flat: A Brief History of the Twenty-first Century by Thomas L. Friedman

A New Earth: Awakening to Your Life's Purpose by Eckhart Tolle

The Secret by Rhonda Byrne

Built to Last: Successful Habits of Visionary Companies by Jim Collins and Jerry L. Porras

Fierce Conversations: Achieving Success at Work and in Life One Conversation at a Time by Susan Scott

Winning by Jack Welch and Suzy Welch

CEO Tools 2.0 by Jim Canfield and Kraig Kramers

Who Moved My Cheese?: An Amazing Way to Deal with Change in Your Work and in Your Life by Spencer Johnson

A Whole New Mind: Why Right-Brainers Will Rule the Future by Daniel H. Pink

Tough Choices: A Memoir by Carly Fiorina

It's Not About the Bike: My Journey Back to Life by Lance Armstrong

The One Minute Manager by Kenneth Blanchard and Spencer Johnson

Think and Grow Rich by Napoleon Hill

APPENDIX D: GLOSSARY

2D: Two-dimensional barcodes normally appear in squares where short bars are placed in rows on top of each other in the shape of a square. They typically contain up to one kilobyte of data and can encode anything that can be digitized, such as photos, signatures, and fingerprints. Examples are PDF 417 and QR Code.

1D: One-dimensional barcodes that contain data in width of symbol rather than height. Examples are EAN, UPC, and Code 39.

AIDC (Automatic Identification and Data Capture): The name of the industry for barcodes and RFID.

ANA: Article Numbering Association (now GS1 UK) performs the same function as UCC for the United Kingdom and Ireland.

Barcode: An optical machine-readable representation of data.

Code 39: An alphanumeric barcode used in the automotive industry and others.

Direct-Thermal Printing: Where no ribbon is present in the printing process.

EAN 13: European Article Number with thirteen digits. This is the type of barcode used globally outside the United States. The extra digit is to identify a greater number of countries; thus 50 is for the United Kingdom, 40 for Germany. The structure is otherwise the same as the UPC.

EAN 128: Used as a standard to encode pallets as part of a global standard in the supply chain. It can encode alphanumeric characters in upper and lower cases as well as ASCII (American Standard Code for Information Interchange) characters which represent text in computers.

Film Master: A piece of transparent film with a barcode plotted to a high degree of accuracy that is used by printers to incorporate with existing artwork for the product label.

GS1: The organization that issues numbers to manufacturers and controls the global database. It issues trading standards based on GTIN (Global Trade Identity Number) and provides the electronic data interface for trading partners.

Hand-Held Terminal (HHT): also known as Portable Data Capture Unit. A device that scans the barcode and is attached to a mobile computer running an application that will prompt the user to enter data. It processes that data and sends it back to the back-office software for further application.

Interleaved 2/5: A numeric-only barcode with wider bars and spaces used to print on corrugated outer containers designed to be more tolerant due to the potential squashing of the corrugation spreading the ink and rendering the code difficult to scan numeric only.

IoT (Internet of Things): Sensors that transmit data 24/7 to the Internet using mobile networks or broadband connecting devices, cars and buildings to exchange data and make real-time business decisions.

ITF-14: Interleaved 2/5 with fourteen digits used to identify a case code or container of multiple consumer units. Structure normally has a 0 to indicate a case code then the EAN 13 with at least one digit changed to differentiate from a multipack.

PDF 417: Portable Data File with four bars and spaces per character each of seventeen modules. Very common for ID cards and driving licenses. See 2D.

Print Contrast Signal: A measurement of the ratio of reflections between the bars and spaces of a symbol, commonly expressed as a percentage. Makes sure correct colors are used for the bars and spaces.

QR Code (Quick Response Code): See 2D. Can be blown up very big and scanned using a mobile phone from a distance. Normally used to link user to a URL with product information. Invented by Japanese car manufacturers to track vehicles in manufacturing.

RFID (Radio Frequency Identification): Uses electromagnetic field to automatically identify and track tags attached to objects. Consists of a silicon chip and some copper wire for an aerial. Active ones can be read long range as they have their own battery. Passive ones are short range and are activated by the reader, which gives them the power. Both types can be enclosed in most types of substrate; for example, paper, plastic, or metal.

Thermal-Transfer Printing: A digital printing process in which material is applied to paper (or some other material) by melting a coating of ribbon so that it stays glued to the material on which the print is applied.

UCC (Uniform Code Council): The numbering authority in the United States that issues manufacturers their unique number to identify each product to keep the integrity of the system, ensuring that each manufactured product is uniquely identified.

UPC (Universal Product Code, later renamed Uniform Product Code): The first barcode used in identifying retail products originating in the United States. It has only twelve digits because when it was developed, the United States was the only country using barcodes, so there was no need to expand it to thirteen digits. See EAN 13.

The structure of the UPC code is as follows:

- Country Code of 0, which means the product, is numbered in the USA or Canada.

- Five digits uniquely allocated to each manufacturer

- Five digits allocated to each SKU (Stock Keeping Unit) by the manufacturer

- One check digit algorithm to ensure no transposition of numbers

Verifier: A device that measures the printed quality of the barcode in terms of correct bar and space width and print contrast signal so that the barcode can scan the first time.

ABOUT THE AUTHOR

Brian Marcel started his career in the London Stock Exchange, but working in an institution didn't suit him, and he got fired from his grandfather's firm. From there, he moved on to sell all types of papers made by Wiggins Teape, a leading British paper manufacturer that sent him to South Africa to enhance his career and learn the art of sales and marketing. It was in Cape Town that he met his wife, Liz, who sadly died of breast cancer after twenty-eight years marriage.

After returning to the United Kingdom, he got involved in the early days of barcoding and soon started his own business selling artwork used for printing barcodes on products. The business expanded, and after the fall of the Berlin Wall in 1989, he set up joint ventures in five of the former Eastern Bloc countries. They are still great success stories in their own right.

Brian was recently married to his new wife, Lisa. He has a daughter, Jessica, that he adopted from Romania. They all live in London.

Raise the Bar, Change the Game is his first book.

Lightning Source UK Ltd.
Milton Keynes UK
UKHW011317020119
334821UK00003B/55/P